TIME OUT, LADIES!

Time Out, Ladies!

Dale Evans Rogers

FLEMING H. REVELL COMPANY
WESTWOOD · NEW JERSEY

Contents

TIME OUT, LADIES!

1

Time Out, Ladies!

I'M NOT QUITE sure what kind of book this will turn out to be, and maybe that's a bad way to start. I hear editors and writers talking about "outlining" a book before you sit down to write: they say the author should have a very clear idea of what he's about to say, and how he will say it, before he puts pen to paper; but if they'll forgive me I'm not going to do it that way at all. This book will just grow, like Topsy in *Uncle Tom's Cabin*, and if it makes as much sense as Topsy made, I'll be satisfied, and I hope you will be, too.

It is going to be a book in which we will discuss some of the problems peculiar to "us women," just as we might discuss them in a coffee break; we'll take time out to think about things that really matter. There are a lot of problems that belong to us rather than to our "mighty men." Yes, I know that the men are supposed to be smarter, and that wives, according to the Bible, should be "in subjection" to their husbands, and that the Bible also holds up Sara, Abraham's wife, as a model ("Even as Sara obeyed Abraham, calling him Lord . . . ," in I PETER

3:6). But if our male lords in general and mine in particular don't mind, I'm going to by-pass them and leave them to gloat in their superiority while I take time out to chat with the mothers, wives, and sweethearts about some things that many men don't seem to know exist, and couldn't do much about if they did know.

I do not want to pose as one who has all the answers; the longer I live the more I realize how little I know. But I think I face most of the problems of the average woman and housewife, even though my career has been something of life in a fishbowl, in the light of almost constant publicity necessary to my work. I know the routine of a big house and a large family; as many of you know, we have had nine youngsters under our roof, and if there is any family problem or crisis that hasn't come our way, I am unaware of it. I write as a mother who has been through the mill, for those now going through it. I've written for teen-agers before this; now I want to chat with the oldsters, with only an occasional talk with the small fry and the teeners. (I wish sometimes that such time-out chats, or coffee breaks, could be made compulsory; without them we women stand a good chance of falling apart. (Many do, nowadays.)

I think it is part of God's plan for all of us to "Come ye yourselves apart . . . and rest a while . . . ," as Jesus said to His disciples(MARK 6:31). Time is of the essence; we have just so much time to do what God put us here to do, and to do it well we need to follow the example of Jesus, who often "sat apart" from the tensions and pressures of life, refreshing Himself in quiet communion with the Father who, He said, was Spirit. We need to get that Spirit into our living. We are like Jesus, at least in this respect: we get tired. He became like us, in His flesh, in order that He might know the problems and the

10

weariness of our flesh, and so help us. (There I go, jumping out ahead of my story already, talking about something I want to discuss carefully in another "break." As Scarlet O'Hara said to Rhett Butler, in *Gone With the Wind*, "Rhett, how you do run on." Well, running on is a *woman's* privilege, and I don't intend to surrender that privilege!)

But this is still a good premise to start with—this knowing that in every problem, every day, Christ is there, sympathetic and understanding and waiting to help. Whatever else I say here, I most want to say that Christ, not I, has the answers. He is *the* answer to every human need. I speak not out of any vain authority of my own, but only for His authority, for in every crisis in my life I have found Him able to do for me what I could not do for myself.

I am indebted to a lot of people for quotes, anecdotes, illustrations, and comments in this book, and I have given credit wherever I can, and I thank them all for helping me to say what I want to say. I am not a professional writer. When things and thoughts come clear to me, I simply write them down, whether they are in sequence or not. And I pause here to thank Dr. Frank S. Mead, Editor-in-Chief of the Fleming H. Revell Company, who has an amazing ability to take these "thoughts-written-at-random" and shuffle and weave them together in sequence. (He didn't want to take this praise but I made him, so there!)

So, for what it's worth—*Time Out, Ladies*—this is what I've found and experienced in the daily living of one wife and mother, and what God and the Bible have done to help me with it all. I hope it may help you, a little. Anyway, thanks for listening!

2

Women!

FIRST, LET'S TAKE time to chat about women.

Women! There is supposed to be something funny about us. James M. Barrie says in one of his books that we weren't made from man's rib, but from his funny bone; the cynic Nietzsche called us "God's second mistake"; old Aristophanes, who was supposed to know everything, said, "There's nothing in the world worse than woman—save some other woman," and modern (male) wisecrackers say, "We can't get along with them, and we can't get along without them." We are supposed to be "the weaker sex." But, sometimes, I wonder. . . .

It is supposed to be funny, but most of it is very unfunny. I doubt that God made woman to play the role of weakling on His earth. I think He had a divine purpose in our creation, and I have Bible evidence for that: "But when the fulness of the time was come, God sent forth his Son, *made of a woman* . . ." (GALATIANS 4:4). And long, long before that, God gave man a helpmeet in Eden because "It is not good that man should be alone . . ." (GENESIS 2:18)—and to bear his children. Without woman—no children, no future generations, no people to inhabit the earth. See anything funny in *that?*

When I was young, I used to resent this idea that as a

woman I was condemned by the men around me to secondary status in God's world. You know, many women actually bemoan the fact that they are women and not men. I did that, before I gave my willful, sinful nature and my stubborn, proud, and rebellious mind over to Christ, and asked Him to come into my heart and mind and give me peace, joy, and purpose—*as a woman.* Having been forced to support myself and my little son at a very early age, I found my embittered self in a man's world, or so I thought, and I resented the fact that men were such "privileged characters" in many of the most important areas of life. They seemed to have all the fun. They could go golfing or hunting or fishing while the poor women were supposed to stay home and take care of the children. I resented the old German idea that woman's province was "cooking, children, and church" —that she was created to work her head off for man's comfort and enjoyment, and never ask for anything better.

I couldn't see it. I allowed that "what was sauce for the goose was sauce for the gander," meaning that a woman should have equal rights and privileges with men, and share their fun. I would throw my shoulders back and try to kid myself into believing that I could go anywhere, do anything, and say anything that a man could do or say. Wasn't I supporting myself and my son by working in this (man's) world? Didn't that make me eligible for something better than simply cooking man's meals and darning his socks?

Then, there was the matter of the double standard. I saw men "cheating" on their wives in illicit "love" affairs, and getting away with it; let a woman try it, and she was condemned by everybody from Boston to Bombay. That riled me. I thought—and still think—that it is not only unfair but disgustingly cruel that the mother is always held responsible for the illegitimate child, while the father goes scot-free. But as I have grown older, and, I hope, a little wiser and a little more compassionate, I have come to see things a bit differently. Now I see that I was not being a true woman in my heart, in this attitude. It is not that I have come to condone the double standard; I still think it wrong. But I have come to understand that it is not up to *me*, either, to condemn either men or women. Who am I to condemn anybody? It is God who is Judge of us all; it is God who is finally to punish or reward: "Vengeance is *mine;* I will repay, saith the Lord" (ROMANS 12:19). I believe that God is no respecter of persons, be they either men or women, when it comes to sin, for both are sinners and both will pay, one by one, for the sins that they commit two by two. I leave it to the mercy and justice of God.

We should learn this lesson from the words and actions of Jesus when the woman taken in adultery was brought before Him. Remember it? He convicted the *men* who wanted to stone that poor woman in His never-to-be-forgotten admonition, "He that is without sin among you, let him first cast a stone at her" (JOHN 8:7). Beautiful! He forgave her. He did not turn away from her in disgust; no, He forgave and strengthened. Can we do less?

I have heard somewhere of a judge who keeps a large stone on his desk, where he cannot miss seeing it while he is considering sentences for the guilty who come before him in court. I like that. . . .

Let us not condemn, or be bitter about all this. Let us set our sights higher. Let us think of why God created woman, what His purpose was. Let's put it this way. God created all of us; ". . . male and female created he them" (GENESIS 1:27) with certain different things in mind. Man was to "have dominion"—he was to struggle for bread, to fight off the dangers that beset us, to do things in a hostile world and environment that woman could not do. But woman He created to do in *her* peculiar strength something that man could not do: to be God's instrument in bringing forth children, to be a help-meet to man, to be the firm power behind the throne of man's dominion, to love, guide, chastise, treasure, bind up a scratch on a little arm, and, better still, to mend a broken heart with that love which is so wonderfully unique in woman. It is a great privilege to be a woman.

The Psalmist says that ". . . the fruit of the womb is his reward" (PSALM 127:3). It is also *our* reward. Just as the tree bears its fruit as it is nourished by the sun and the rain sent of God; just as, when the time has come and the fruit is ripe, the tree releases its fruit to be used of God in strengthening the bodies of His people, so is woman beautiful when she releases her child into God's care and service.

If we refuse to let go and let God have His way with us and our children, we are cheating God and depriving the children of the chance to grow and mature, to grow "in wisdom and stature, and in favour with God and man" (LUKE 2:52).

So men and women are different. God knew what He was doing when He made us so. He made no two of us alike. Even the most "look-alike" twins are different: it may be only in different color in the hair or the eyes, in physical stature, in one preferring coffee to tea, or in preferring a date to a night with the schoolbooks; but

16

they are different. Each child is different, each has his own pattern, and only God knows what that pattern is, for He designed it. And only when parents turn to Him to determine the pattern can they rightly train up the child in the way he should go. What a responsibility—especially for the mother, who has far more influence in this department than the father has! Our children must see the peace, the wisdom, the understanding, the love and justice of the Lord Jesus Christ in us, their mothers.

So, understanding this, I have come to believe that it is a privilege, and never a handicap, to be a woman. I don't mind, any more, being reminded that, as a woman, I am "one of man's ribs." I think the Lord must have picked the rib because it was the bone closest to man's heart. I also think He must have picked the strongest rib man had for this purpose, because women can endure so much that men cannot. Can you imagine most men bearing up under the pain of childbirth? Have you ever noticed how helpless most men seem to be with the ordinary aches and pains? When I see them in sickness, I am sure that women were fashioned with more resiliency, since God knew they were to bring the race into being and to heal the hurts of the children of men. I'm sorry Eve sinned, and that she tempted Adam, but I sure am glad that God allowed her to become a mother. To me, that is the greatest joy in life.

You know, ladies, a woman is mother to her husband as well as to her children. With all due respect, may I say that to me a man is a grown-up boy who never quite ceases to *be* a boy. Girls mature much faster emotionally, as a rule, than boys. Is that because they have a divine, built-in "mother instinct"? Boys are out hunting lizards and snakes, or trying to catch a frog on a hook covered by a bread-crumb or a piece of red flannel while girls are playing house and talking to their dolls just as a full-grown mother talks to her baby. That is no accident; I believe God planned it that way.

On the other hand, boys have qualities that are marvelous, necessary, and delightful. The minute they learn to ride a bicycle they get a job delivering newspapers or bread for the local grocery store; they are born providers, and they learn at a very early age to provide for and protect the home. They are as proud as Punch when they come home with a string of fish (even when they are goldfish) for supper.

Isn't God wonderful, in His creative artistry! He has thought of everything—of boys to provide, of women to love and comfort and encourage the man. Who else but God could have planned it so well?

Right now, I wish you ladies would open your Bibles to the thirty-first chapter of Proverbs, and stop whatever you are doing and just sit down and read it and think about it—think it through. Solomon is said to have written it, but sometimes I wonder if a woman didn't write it, for as a description of the good and worthy woman it says a lot of things that I believe only a woman could say. Start with verse 11: "The heart of her husband doth safely trust in her. . . ." (Good homes are founded on trust and faith; without them, there is confusion, and maybe divorce.) "She . . . worketh willingly with her hands" (v. 13). (She does the million and one things that make a house a home, and she does it in love.) "She is like the merchants' ships; she bringeth her food from afar" (v. 14). (She brings heaven to earth, brings to her children the habit of prayer, a consciousness of God.) "She riseth also while it is yet night, . . . her candle goeth not out by night" (vv. 15, 18). (Babies cry for their mothers when they fear the dark; the mother is the nurse.) "She stretcheth out her hand to the poor . . ." (v. 20). (She has a hand in all sorts of projects for community welfare; without her, I think, the missionary enterprise would die!) ". . . in her tongue is the law of kindness . . ." (v. 26). (Men are stern with justice, often brutal with it; mercy is the forte of women.) "Her children arise up, and call her blessed . . ." (v. 28). (It is a rare man who will say ill of his mother, even when she deserves it!)

Yes, it is a blessed thing to be a woman.

Now, lest I seem to be too hard on the men and the fathers, let me say this: father has his part to play, and it is a big part, and we have never quite given him credit for it. We seem to think that it is his duty to work away the years of his life to provide food and shelter and education for his children. We have been kidding too long about "Father should bring home the bacon," and far too long we have been looking at him as a sort of star boarder in the home. We allow our children to call him "the old man," and, if truth be told, neither we nor our children give him the respect that he deserves. I'm not poking fun at him while I sing praises for the ladies, but I am saying that God was everlastingly right in concluding that man could not live without woman, and then He created woman to complement, to *complete* man. We are man's intuition, his gentleness, his restraining power, his compassion. My Bible says that ". . . the woman is the glory of the man" (that's in I CORINTHIANS 11:7), and I think that describes it well.

Or you might say that woman is the "Whoa!" part of man. Woman! Have you read that little poem by Mary Caroline Davies?

Women are door-mats and have been;
The years those mats applaud—
They keep their men from going in
With muddy feet to God.

I refuse to take this door-mat business too literally because I don't like the idea of being pushed around or "walked on" by anybody, but I don't believe that's what the poet was getting at. She meant that women were created of God to be the cleansing, ennobling, uplifting part of the human race and family. Men have to fight their way in a pretty rough world, and they become rough as they fight; but when they want the lovelier, gentler, more inspiring things of life, they turn to woman. She says "Whoa!" to the lower urges of human existence, and sets high the standards for her children. That's why the children rise to bless her.

No, all women are not like this—but with Christ they *can* be. We are truly women, in the highest degree, when we belong to Him. When we do not belong to Him and allow Him to give us guidance, things get out of focus, and there is confusion, and in the confusion we are less than we should be, as women, and we do not present a true picture of ourselves. Our true personalities are covered with a mask; we throw up a facade, and try to be something we are not, something not at all admirable.

God's original creation is beautiful: *let's keep it that way!* He made us not as "the weaker sex," but as the gentler part; *let us cultivate the gentleness of Christ in our characters.* You girls, growing now into the full status of womanhood, listen to me, please. Serve God *and* your children; see to it that God is in your children, *and that they know it.*

20

During the last war we saw an Army poster with a picture of Uncle Sam pointing a long finger at the young men of the country, and under the picture was the slogan, "Uncle Sam needs men!" In a higher sense, I think there never was a time when this country had greater need of *Christian* men, and by and large the development of Christian character in the boys who become men is the job of the Christian woman and mother. Woman is the backbone of the family and the nation.

Dare to do it. Get a conviction about it, and stick to it. Never mind what the crowd says; never mind "what most women do." Someone has said that if he always thought as the crowd thinks, he'd think he was wrong. Crowds are often stupid in their ridicule of the Christian woman. They simply do not know. If you know the right way, the Christian way, then walk in it and let your children grow up in it as you grow in wisdom and faith and knowledge of Christ's Way.

It isn't easy, this growing up. I know, for I was a teen-ager once, even if my own children seem to find it hard to believe! One of them said to me not long ago, "Mom, before you got *old.* . . ." Hmmm! Frankly, I do not feel old, and unless I compare a photograph taken years ago with one taken yesterday, I don't feel that I have changed at all. Oh, yes, I do realize it some mornings when I don't spring out of bed with quite the zip I had a few years ago, and whereas I used to hate going to bed at all, now I find my comfortable mattress and a good book delightful. Each year I notice a few new aches and pains, but—believe me—I wouldn't turn back the clock for anything. (I can just hear some of you saying, "Oh, yeah?") I know. When I was as young as you are, the thought of age horrified me. At twenty I was using a magnifying glass to look for those tell-tale crow's feet around my eyes. When I turned thirty, I thought, "Well, I may as well go pick out my shroud." Then, when I reached thirty-five, Christ came into my life, and age "went by the boards," and I found that age was a matter of an attitude of mind and heart.

Time has become eternity to me—a Christ-filled eternity, in which the word "age" is never mentioned.

3
Marriage

MARRIAGE IS THE one subject we women are sure to think about and worry about, whatever else we do. I don't think I have ever met a woman who, in her heart, didn't want to get married, even though she may tell you that she wouldn't care if she never saw another man in her life. Marriage is the great and shining hour of the life of woman—and it is the trickiest, most dangerous and fateful moment of her life, too. She can make or break her whole existence when she says, "I do."

Some call it life's greatest lottery. Marriage *can* be that, if we are fools enough to think of it as a lottery or a gamble, or to comfort ourselves with the thought, as some poor women do, that "I can get a divorce and get out of it, if I don't like it." If you want to smash your life to bits, that's a good philosophy. But if you want to know one shining hour after another, all your life long, try the Christian approach to marriage.

I think the best advice I have ever heard about getting married came from the late beloved Dr. Henrietta Mears, who did such an amazing job as Director of Religious Education at Hollywood Presbyterian Church. A very dear young friend of mine, Judy Whisenant, came to work at the church after graduation from high school and some work in college; she and her family were neighbors when Roy and I married and came to live in Hollywood Hills. I knew her as a girl who was very serious about life, and about her commitment to Christ. After some time working in the church office, she took a job as an airline hostess, and it was then that she met young David Whisenant, who is now working with youth in church and studying for the ministry. While Judy was trying to make up her mind about David, she surely heard the words of advice that Henrietta Mears often gave to young people in the "considering" stage: "Don't go out with a person you couldn't think of marrying—you may!" She also advised, "Be willing to give all your life to the Lord, even the most difficult part of it—your *dating* life." This will have its effect upon your whole life. Don't settle for second best: the Lord will have His first best ready for you, if you are willing to wait. Judy waited. She made *sure*. She took no "leap in the dark." Her marriage to David, when it came, was no lottery. She *knew*. David was her man. David, like Judy, was a Christian, and wanted God's will in his life. They were married, *and it has worked*.

That's Point One about getting married: the time to determine what your marriage is to be is the time you start dating.

Point Two: Understand that marriage is not always a matter of romance, of moonlight and roses. Differences will come. There will be arguments. If they do not come, something is *wrong*. I remember hearing the story of a bishop who attended a dinner at which an old man got up and said that in his thirty years of marriage, he and his wife had never had an argument. The bishop got up and said, "Now there are two things to keep clear about that statement. First, that it probably isn't true; second, if it *is* true, how ghastly!" I agree with the bishop. Troubles will come in *any* marriage; I think it is a part of God's plan and testing that they come.

Trouble came to Judy and David: they lost their first-born son, little Samuel, who graced this vale of tears for just eighteen hours. Some marriages break up after such an experience, for the simple reason that the father and mother are not spiritually prepared for it. Not this marriage! Little Sam's parents had read, and they remembered, the Scripture which tells us that ". . . all things work together for good to them that love *God*, to them who are the called according to his purpose" (ROMANS 8:28). There was a purpose in his death, just as Roy and I found purpose in the deaths of our three children. David and Judy did not sit down and wring their hands and ask, "Why should this happen to *us?*" They accepted it as right that little Sam's soul should return to God, and that the eyes and hearts of his parents should be pulled in His direction through his going. In other words, they trusted completely in God in every grief and joy that came to their marriage; they knew that God must have had great confidence in their spiritual strength.

The other day I had a letter from Judy. Here is one line of it: "If a child of God marries a child of the devil, then the child of God will doubtless have troubles with his father-in-law!" Beautiful, isn't it?

Yes, God had a lot of confidence in the spiritual strength of David and Judy. He knows what we should know: that given this spiritual strength and understanding, marriage never breaks up in divorce. Those couples married in church, the statisticians tell us, stand a far better chance of making a go of it than do those couples married before a justice of the peace; that's because the Spirit is given a chance to *make* it work out. There are times, I suppose (or so the judges and the marriage counselors say), when a marriage becomes so absolutely hopeless that divorce is the only way out. Every marriage is different. But even in the worst of marriages, with the help of good counseling with a minister (and prayer, prayer, *prayer*) divorce can be avoided and a happy relationship established. I think it's all a matter of the Spirit in the heart. Jesus was quite definite about this. He said, "Moses because of the hardness of your hearts suffered you to put away your wives: but from the beginning it was not so" (MATTHEW 19:8) You see, divorce was *permitted*, but it was never God's purpose.

How I wish I might have had Judy's early Christian commitment; how I wish that her spiritual strength and trust in God had been in me at the time of my first marriage. Had it been, had I been a true Christian then, I would never have had to face that dismal experience of divorce. But my son's father wanted his freedom, and my pride was hurt, and so it happened. Had I been a Christian, in the first place, I would not have defied my parents and eloped in my early teens. Certainly, when I married, I would have made sure that both the man and I stood together, eye to eye and shoulder to shoulder in our responsibility to the Lord and to the child involved. Nothing "worked" for me in those days, because I wouldn't let the Lord work His way in my heart.

But now it does work and nothing is so important as the "now." *Now* is all we really have—not yesterday, nor tomorrow, but now. ". . . now is the accepted time . . . now is the day of salvation" (II CORINTHIANS 6:2). It is never too late to make a marriage work, to turn to Christ to be forgiven and strengthened, and to start again.

I know whereof I speak, for I have been through it—through hasty, ill-considered, un-Christian marriage, disillusionment, separation, divorce—but thanks be to God, He finally got through to me, and my heart had its hardness taken away, and my life transformed, and I have known the joy of *a real* marriage. I know now that divorce settles nothing, but that God binding the hearts of man and wife together can settle *anything*.

I was thinking about that the other day when the awning on my trailer blew away. (I often run away from telephones and tensions to do my writing in a trailer parked near a beach.) The thing just took up and off, and I thought for a minute that the whole trailer and everything in it, including me, would land in the Pacific. The wind was strong, and the man who set up the awning hadn't driven its poles deep enough into the ground, and off it went. Marriages often take off and up for the same reason: they are not grounded deeply enough in God's Word and in prayer. When the storms come, they are uprooted. This is why marriages based on a slender faith have such a slim chance of happiness, of growth, and even of plain survival. The surest way to lose a mate is to clutch him and not give him a chance to breathe or to be an individual in his own right. The surest way to lose the love and respect of a child is to do the same thing with him.

This brings me to the point of in-laws' cooperation or interference in the marriages of their children. A domestic-relations-court judge said recently that he could find in-law trouble behind seventy-five percent of our American divorces. We should have sense enough to let our children *go* when they marry. When the preacher says, "I pronounce you man and wife," a new family has begun, and it does *not* include Mamma and Papa! So many well-meaning mothers and fathers do not seem to realize that they are jeopardizing the marriages of their children in offering constant unasked-for advice, or in demanding constant attention to themselves. We older folks have had our day; why can't we let the kids have theirs? Let's be slow to criticize (Lord, help us to use our ears more than our mouths!), quick to praise, to encourage. Let's ask if it is *convenient* for us to come and visit.

I don't know about you, but when my children are happy, I am happy. There are so many things a father-in-law or a mother-in-law can do to be happy without encroaching upon the privacy of their married children. We should always be ready to help in time of trouble, but never to play the judge in time of marital disputes. Let us remember that "Those whom God hath joined together, let no man put asunder." Let not woman put asunder, either.

We have told our children that they are not to come running home to Mother and Dad whenever they have an argument; we do not want to be responsible for a break-up in their marriage. One of our children called up one day and demanded, "Mom, come and get me; we've had a fight and I am not going to stay here another minute!" Just like that! I said, "No, I will not come to get you. You stay there and work it out. When you've done that, I'll come over." And I hung up. They made it, and made up, and this child has never called me a second time with such a request. Was I hard, unfeeling? I don't think so. It is entirely too easy these days to get divorces; people get them because Father likes Wheaties and Mother likes oatmeal, and so they are "incompatible"! Too many youngsters refuse even to try to work their marriage out like sensible human beings.

I think we encourage this when, as children, we allow them to start their little projects, half-finish them, and rush off on another project, leaving the thing half finished. This is the butterfly technique, flitting from one flower to another, taking a little here and a little there, and forever, restlessly, moving on. It may be all right for butterflies, but not for human beings. The problem and the butterfly shiftiness are complicated by the fact that we parents, too, are so busy with our precious little projects that we do the same thing. Our children see their failings in us! My friend Judy has a word for that one; she thinks that "children ought to have more models and fewer critics." She's right. What a responsibility we have! How can our children be good marriage partners unless they've seen good marriage partners in Dad and Mother?

4

The Christian Wife

HERE IS SOMETHING for us wives to think about. I haven't any idea who wrote it, or where it came from; a good friend sent it along to me after she had read it. If some of you ladies have heard it and know its source, please let me know, will you?

It bears the simple and intriguing title. *Beatitudes of a Christian Wife*. Here it is:

"Blessed is she whose daily tasks are a labor of love, for willing hands and a happy heart translate beauty into a privilege and her labor becomes a service to God and to those she loves.

"Blessed is she who opens the door to welcome both stranger and well-loved friend, for gracious hospitality is a test of true Christianity and spiritual stewardship.

"Blessed is she who mends stockings and toys and broken hearts, for her understanding is a balm to those in need.

"Blessed is she who scours and scrubs. She knows that cleanliness is important, but that forgiveness of sin in the human heart can only be purified through the blood of Jesus Christ.

"Blessed is she whom children love, for the love of a child is more to be valued than fame and fortune.

"Blessed is she who sings at her work, for music lightens the heaviest load and brightens the dullest chore.

"Blessed is she who dusts away doubt and fear, and sweeps out the cobwebs of confusion, for her faith in Christ will triumph over all adversity, and her patience of hope will be rewarded by the Lord.

"Blessed is she who serves laughter and smiles with every meal, for her buoyancy of spirit is an aid to mental and physical digestion. The Bible says, 'A merry heart doeth good like a medicine.'

"Blessed is she who preserves the sanctity of the Christian home, for hers is a sacred trust that crowns her with dignity, and results in her children arising and calling her blessed, and her husband praising her also."

Source unknown

May I speak plainly? We are in a bad way as a nation because our homes are in a bad way. The old, stern hand of Christian discipline has relaxed, if not disappeared. It just may be true that "the hand that rocks the cradle rules the world"; there is more truth than fiction in that when you listen to the tributes of great men to their mothers. But it is also true that the same hand can *destroy* the world by indifference to the responsibility given to women at the hand of Almighty God. At whose knee does a child first learn? The Roman Catholic Church, I am told, says in effect, "Give us a child until he is seven and he will always be a Catholic." That church understands the importance of the early impressionable years. My good friend, Rev. Harley Wright Smith, is a minister in the Protestant Episcopal Church; he said not long ago that it is generally agreed among top men in child welfare work and psychologists that a child feels either acceptance or rejection practically at birth—that the baby is sensitive that early to the vibrations of love or nonlove about him.

I think that must be right. Comforting as other arms may be, there are no arms like mother's. This I have reason, good personal reason, to believe. I also believe that *any* woman's arms are blessed to *any* child. I thank God for women who have love enough in their arms to take other women's children and cuddle them as their own. Any child you take for your own becomes your own if you give of yourself to a child. So may I suggest to that legion of bored wives and housewives who have been denied the privilege of children of their own that they try holding some lonely, motherless child in their arms? Listen, ladies: I am not boasting or patting myself on the back when I say that I have tried it, and that I have found joy in it. I have had two of my own natural children and seven other children by adoption, and they are all my children, equally beloved and precious.

How much trouble would be averted if more childless mothers gave their frustrated love to motherless children! A boy was executed for murder in a state prison not long ago; when the warden told him it was just barely possible that the sentence could be commuted to life imprisonment, the boy said, "Skip it, warden. I've had enough of life. I never had a decent home to live in; my father was a drunk and my mother was worse, and they kicked me out. *Nobody ever wanted me, and nobody wants me now!*"

Dean Farrar said once, "If we work upon marble, it will perish; if we work upon stone, it will crumble to dust; but if we take a child and train it well, we rear a monument which time can never efface."

See what I mean?

5

Children

I ALMOST DID not write this chapter; it seemed just
too much to try to write *one* chapter on children and
say all I want to say. I could hardly say that in a whole
book! So you'll understand, at the start, why I am not
attempting here to cover all the problems we mothers
face with our offspring. That wouldn't make sense,
because, first of all, there isn't room in this book to
do that, and, second, because I hesitate to tell every
mother what to do with every child. I've had some experience with my rather large brood, and I simply want to
pass on two or three things I think of paramount importance.

Most of us *want* children; we are not like that movie
star who said that she refused to bring children into such
a savage world as ours, to slave and sacrifice for them,
and then see them destroyed in another world war.
There aren't very many women who share her opinion.
Most of us are like the childless Rachel of Old Testament
days who cried out to her husband, "Give me children,
or else I die" (GENESIS 30:1). Sure, when they come, and
when at times they drive us nearly frantic, we are
tempted to cry out that we'll die trying to take care of
them, but we forget all that when they put their arms

around our necks, or come running with a skinned knee. We *want* children, in spite of all the heartaches they bring with them.

I have often wished that they might bring with them, when they are born, a prenatal instruction in the dictum laid down by Paul in EPHESIANS 6:1—"Children, obey your parents. . . ." Insofar as we know, Paul had no children, but he sure knew what he was talking about when he said *that!* "Children, obey your parents *in the Lord.* . . ." The Lord is the Creator of parents, and He meant them to be obeyed, but as I look around me I think not only the children, but many of the parents as well, either do not know of this Pauline counsel, or deliberately ignore it if they do. Obedience seems to be something that passed out with the one-hoss shay and kerosene lamps—something our fathers and mothers knew, but passé and old fashioned now. Look around for yourself. Listen to some of the "child experts" who tell mothers that they must not "inhibit" their children in forcing them to do *anything.* All due credit to them, I think these expert child psychologists and "liberal" educators have done us a great disservice and a lot of harm. One psychologist who once felt this way has changed his mind; he says that he is appalled at the thought that this philosophy of noninterference on the part of parents has given us "a generation of selfish, hard-boiled little monsters." His language may be too strong, but his basic idea is correct. Modern youth—at least a *lot* of modern youths—frighten me, with their undisciplined violence, more than the threat of nuclear destruction frightens me. The nuclear bomb is a *material* threat; the lack of discipline in youth is a *moral* and *spiritual* threat.

The disrespect of children large and small is sickening,

and it is as much the fault of us parents as it is theirs. We parents find it so easy, in an argument over right and wrong with our children, to just give up and say, "Oh, all *right*—go ahead," instead of standing firm for what we know is right. Too many mothers are like the cook in one household who gave the young son of the household some spoiled peas to eat, just because he "wanted" them, and in spite of the mother's order that he should not have them. He wanted them, so—we mustn't *inhibit* him!

Often a mother will say, "My child won't love me if I'm a square, if I'm too strict." Listen, ladies, a child *wants* to be told "No!" lots of times. Okay, so you're a "heavy" with his young friends, and he says you're awful in making him do things that other mothers never make their sons do, but inwardly he will respect you when you stand pat and don't give in to his every whim and wish. I heard lately of one parent whose teen-age son was picked up with some of his pals for a Hallowe'en prank; a policeman brought him home, and the parents really let that boy have it; he didn't get out again that Hallowe'en. But a day or so later he was astounded to hear that the parents of the other boys in the crowd had said to their sons, "Oh, well, boys will be boys. Go on out and enjoy yourselves!" And we wonder why the rise in juvenile delinquency—and why we have so many gangsters!

I plead guilty to an occasional retreat into this "Oh, well" philosophy, and I have always found it a rough road to travel, later on. God says "No" to us many, many times in life. He has been saying it for centuries. When a thing is wrong, He shouts "No!" and if we disobey, we pay for it. It never fails.

If I had ever dared talk to my parents, as a child, as I hear many children talking today, I wouldn't have been able to sit down for a week! Someone has said that "More board meetings in the woodshed would produce fewer cases in the juvenile courts." He's right, whoever he is. The time to start building respect into children is when they are babies. The time to start saying "No," and meaning it, is when the baby tries to put your pincushion in his mouth. The word "No" is a health-building word. You wouldn't dream of saying "Yes" to a child who wanted to stick his finger in an electric socket, would you? Yet you allow him to "express" himself in rebellion all through babyhood, childhood, and teenhood, and when you do that you really shouldn't be surprised to see him end up in the electric chair, where his "self-expression" is sadly and definitely ended.

Strong talk? Strong subject. Let's quit this pussy-footing, ladies, and act like *women!* Let's *mean* "No" when we say "No." *But let us say it in love,* never in frustration or in a fit of uncontrolled temper. I have just quoted Paul, in EPHESIANS 6. Let me quote him again, in the same chapter: "And, ye fathers [he might have said 'Mothers'], provoke not your children to wrath . . ." (v. 4). Try to understand their problems before you reach for the hairbrush. Their problems are as important to them as ours are to us.

God loves us. He disciplines us in love. He loves us so much that He became one of us in order to teach us, and finally to redeem us, at a terrible cost to Himself. Why don't we follow Him, we mothers who call ourselves Christians? Why don't we teach our children that our own Saviour was subject to His parents (LUKE 2:51), according to the commandment that a child should honor his father and his mother? If He honored His parents and was "subject" to them, then surely our children should know it and have the benefit of His example. He should be their pattern—*before* there comes the necessity of the board meeting in the woodshed.

Will you forgive a personal reference? I was shopping one day in a large department store when I heard a little tyrant, aged about four, screaming to her mother at the top of her lungs, "I don't like you! I don't like you!" It was pathetic. The mother was so embarrassed that she walked out ahead of the child in an effort to convince the gaping people around her that this wasn't *her* child! Pathetic, and, to me, infuriating. While the child screamed her hatred, the mother calmly stopped to price some dress-goods on a counter. I wondered what was going on inside that mother; it certainly couldn't have been what was going on inside me. If I had been in her place, I muttered to myself . . .!

And then it happened to *me*. One of my own got to screaming—not that she didn't like me or love me, but that she was denied something she wanted to do—in public. Dodie was about two years old when it happened. We were shopping in a supermarket, and while I was busy at the check-out counter, Dodie suddenly decided that she wanted some chewing gum which she had spotted on the shelf beside the cash register. I said to her, "No, Dodie, not yet. Not until the lady has finished checking us out." That didn't register with Dodie, who wanted what she wanted *right now*. She threw herself down on the cement floor and went into a howling Choctaw tirade that stopped everybody in the place and made them turn around to see what was the matter with the poor child. I knew what was the matter, better than they did. This was childish temper, and it had to be controlled. I said to the checking lady and to the folks behind me, "Excuse me, for just a minute," grabbed Dodie up off the floor, turned up her posterior and practiced a laying on of hands that was not quite spiritual—or *was* it? She yelled bloody murder; it must have been heard in Timbucktoo. But never, never again did she try it, and now she is fourteen years old.

You say it was undignified, and perhaps it was. I certainly didn't enjoy it, any more than she did. An elderly lady behind me was horrified; she sniffed loudly and said, "The very idea!" I tried to hold my temper as she looked at me as though I were some kind of prehistoric monster, and I managed to control it enough to say, "Yes, ma'am, that's the idea!" She sniffed again and walked away, looking daggers at me over her shoulder.

No, I didn't enjoy it, but I felt that I had to do it. Dodie was a strong-willed child and she just had to learn, and this was the perfect psychological moment for her to learn, that our own will is not the only will that is to be obeyed. I was a strong-willed child, too, and that strong will had become both an asset and a liability to me, and I was anxious to spare Dodie the tragedy of uncontrolled will that had nearly wrecked my life. Believe it or not, that affair in the supermarket was a love affair.

But let me get this straight, and I hope you get it straight: this was the only time this sort of thing had happened or was ever to happen. When I suggest such a firm hand, I am not suggesting that it is the only method of saving our children from the tragedies of disobedience. I think there is a lot to be done before that happens, if it has to happen. I think that, first of all, the *parent*, mother or father, must himself or herself be subject to God's will in trying to live, by His grace, according to His will, and must be setting every day and every hour the very best example possible in the eyes of the child. There is an old axiom (Emerson said it first, I think) to the effect that "What you *are* speaks so loud that I cannot hear what you say." If we tell our children not to do something because it is wrong for them to do it, then we should not do it, either. The best teaching is example. Words are easy, deeds are hard, but deeds get the job done. It's like looking furtively in the rear-view mirror of your car, when you're about to violate a traffic law, to make sure there isn't a cop on the corner who may see you do it and call you down or give you a ticket. Do you think the child beside you on the seat doesn't see that, and know what you're doing? Think again. Do you really think you can tell your child not to cheat, and then let him hear you tell Jim Jones, your nextdoor neighbor, of how you finagled the figures on your income-tax form and cheated Uncle Sam out of fifty bucks? You think the children don't notice, that they don't store it all up in their little minds? Believe you me, they do. If they are old enough to understand, they know when you're a hypocrite, when you're doing something that you've told them they musn't do "because it's wrong." They will look at you with disturbing eyes when you turn from the income-tax blank to read to them from the Scriptures, "Render unto Caesar that which is Caesar's, and . . ."

In other words, you can preach to them until you are blue in the face, but until they see you practice what you're preaching, you had better say nothing at all. You may demand that they respect your authority, but they know in their little hearts and minds that you are not obeying God's authority—and in their eyes, you haven't any authority worth mentioning.

Yes, the Bible tells the child to obey his parents, and he

must, because God commands it in His Word. That is His plan for the human family. But never let us forget that God demanded that we adults obey Him and His will, and respect His authority over us, before we make a similar demand of our children. God has as little respect for a disobedient father or mother as He has for a disobedient child. We must give the child love before we give him the rod. We must lead him in love. Now that we have taken God out of the public schools (we'll be saying a lot more of this, later), the whole burden of spiritual guidance and development falls squarely upon the home and the church, and we parents had better "get on the ball."

6
Day In,
Day Out

I HEAR A lot of women complaining about the drudgery of housework. They say, "It's the monotony that gets you down," or "It's the routine, doing the same thing over and over, day in, day out." There's many a woman who can see nothing glamorous or romantic in washing dishes or running the vacuum cleaner.

But it doesn't bore me, and it doesn't get me down. I've found a way to lick it.

Take an average morning in my life as mother and lady-boss of Double-R Bar Ranch. This morning I was up at six. It was a gloriously beautiful California morning. I walked into the kitchen—where I would be spending the next few hours in the first motions of the daily routine—and looked out of the window, and immediately I felt like singing. The beauty of God was in all the earth and sky, and in every common little bush and tall pine and distant mountain; they all seemed to be singing together of the glory of God. I thought of that line in Solomon's Song (2:12), ". . . the time of the singing of birds is come . . . ," as I watched the sparrows and other birds flit from tree to tree and soar off into the sky in sheer joy at being able to live and fly, and I heard their laughter and their chatter, and I laughed with them. I know you may not have such a view from your window, but you have some sort of view, and if you take time to look at it you will see the glory of God in it, and you will hear the sound of *His* music. I wonder why so many women miss it!

I saw and heard all this at the start of another day, and my heart was light with it as I reached for cups and plates and the package of cereal on the shelf, and my kitchen was bright and good. The joy of God's creation was there, and it filled my being. Samuel Rutherford said in his dungeon cell, "This morning God spoke to me, and my cell was ablaze with light!"

The sun climbed over the hilltop a mile away, red as the ripe pomegranate in our front yard. As much as I growl at the six-o'clock alarm that gets me up, by the time I get breakfast started for the family I am glad to be alive in the throbbing world about me.

We have a firm morning schedule in our house: breakfast at 6:30, pack lunch for Dodie, Dusty takes off at 7:15 for high school, and Dodie is driven to junior high school. After the last slam of the door (sometimes I think they have a regular schedule for slamming every door in the house, and they never miss one!)—after the last slam, Mama sits down to a cup of coffee and surveys her echoing domain. It's time now for her to read some Scripture, to think a moment on her blessings, and to ask God's help for the long day ahead. I wouldn't dream of starting the day without that; I couldn't get through the rest of the day without it. I have long since learned to take one day at a time, to take one step at a time and trust God for the next, and to know that without God all through my day, I might not have tomorrow.

Have you ever stopped to think of what you would do if God were to tell you that you had just one more day to live? Someone asked St. Francis about that, and he replied, "I would go on hoeing my garden." I like that. I like starting the day with God in prayer and meditation. It's a good idea to do what the old Negro preacher says he did when he was asked the secret of his good preaching; he said, "I jest stays prayed up."

I get through the dish-washing and the cleaning-up, and while I'm at it I often repeat that little poem of Klara Munkers about the pots and pans. Do you know it? It goes:

Lord of all pots and pans and things, since I've not time to be
  A saint by doing lovely things or watching late with Thee,
Or dreaming in the dawn light or storming Heaven's gates
  Make me a saint by getting meals and washing up the plates.
Although I must have Martha's hands, I have a Mary mind,
  And when I black the boots and shoes, Thy sandals, Lord, I find.
I think of how they trod the earth, what time I scrub the floor.
  Accept this meditation, Lord, I haven't time for more.
Warm all the kitchen with Thy love, and light it with Thy peace;

Forgive me all my worrying and make my grumbling
cease.
Thou who didst love to give men food, in room or by
the sea,
Accept this service that I do, I do it unto Thee.

After devotional time I try to snatch a few minutes for
a walk up the mountain behind our house, to "the rock."
It's *my* rock, and God's; He put it there for me to enjoy.
It is a big stone, flat on the top, overlooking Chatsworth
Lake. On clear days, I can see for miles in every direction from my rock, and sometimes I just sit there drink-
ing in the beauty all around, feeling my heart grow
warm with gratitude for the goodness of the God who
created it. Other times, I stretch out flat on the rock,
close my eyes and let Him clear away the confusion of
my mind and let the warmth of the sun sink into me. I
try to think of nothing in particular, but simply wait for
the still, small voice to speak. Sometimes it speaks so
clearly and deeply that real inspiration comes, and I want
to leap up and run back to the house and write it down,
or talk about it in my heart, or just get busy, busy, busy.
Other times, like today, I just rest and go leisurely
back.

On my way back this particular morning I stumbled
into a thorn bush; I was about to sound off in resentment
at the thorn sticking to my ankle, when I looked at the
bush and saw something I had never seen before. Surrounded by the pesky burrs, right in the middle of the
bush, was a tall stem with a burst of wood roses growing
on its little branches. I had just returned from Hawaii,
where I had seen wood roses growing everywhere, and
where the people use them so imaginatively in their

homes, and now I was as happy as a child at the thought of finding one on our ranch—of all places, right in the middle of a thorn bush! Maybe that's where all wood roses come from; that thought struck a chord deep inside. Thorn bushes are no fun to tangle with, but this little wood rose had a special kind of beauty surrounded by thorns. It's like the answers we get from the tragedies of life, I thought: the tragedies may hurt, as the thorns hurt, yet there is real beauty in the lessons we learn from them. God's ways are high above our ways; He can, and does, bring beauty and good out of deepest sorrow, if we will only take time to look for the blossoms. I braved the thorns to pick a handful of the bright flowers to place on our mantel beside the photographs of Robin, Debbie, and Sandy, our three angels.

I have another "quiet spot" in addition to my rock; my altar and chapel. A friend of mine gave me an old-fashioned kneeling-bench, and many a time, when the pressure becomes almost more than I can bear, that hallowed little altar has been a place of refuge and a re-fueling station. I use it when I haven't time to climb up to my rock. I always find God there, waiting for me to come. He will always be there, always at the little altar, and it strengthens me to know that. Of course, the whole house is His—but that little altar and kneeling-bench are especially set aside for Him, and for me, and for our quiet communion together. Do you have an altar in your house? You could—just one corner that is dedicated to God, where His Book is always open.

I walk into the living room, and consider the furniture. We have quite an assortment of furniture in our house. I think that any respectable interior decorator might have a heart attack just by looking at it, but it's home, sweet home, to us, and I don't care very much what the interior decorators may think of it. It holds what we cherish —Roy, the children, and I. Father likes longhorns, and so we have longhorns over the big fireplace and in several other conspicuous places in the house. I like pictures, and I have far too many of them. I have pictures for which there is no room on the walls. Some day, maybe, I'll hang them. They are good to have around.

I am one of those housewives who is forever re-arranging furniture; I am what you might call "a compulsive furniture-mover." Roy is very patient about it, but he does occasionally complain that he never knows where to sit down. But I love moving the stuff around. I think it's good to rearrange things in a house, just as it's good to rearrange things and thoughts in our lives. It's good to go to a different church, now and then, to worship in a different setting, and to see how others honor God in the arrangements of their sanctuaries. To live shut in by one set of spiritual "furniture" seems to me to be asking for spiritual claustrophobia; we need a fresh look, now and then.

So I get at it, move things around, clean up, dust, sweep, put new flowers in the vase. Most of it I love, for this is my castle. To be honest, some of it I despise. I hate such chores as cleaning a stove; I don't like to spend hours over an ironing-board. But, you know, I've found that some people can even like ironing? Our Scottish foster-daughter, Marion, tells me that she and a friend next door iron together, and chat while they're doing it. And there is always the possibility of a coffee break, which is about now, for me.

I think often about two references to the house and the home in the Bible. One is found in JOSHUA 24:15, in which the old warrior Joshua lays down the law, ". . . but as for me and my house, we will serve the Lord." A warrior—especially a warrior so faithful to God—would say that. It is good to ponder but, frankly, sometimes I think there is a little too much of the military dictator in it. I have known homes in which a stern and almost forbidding religion was forced on the children of the house, and somehow I do not like it. I think religion should be a wholehearted, voluntary thing, not something commanded by the parents. I agree with good old Joshua enough to see that there is worship in our house, but I insist that it be a joyous and not a command performance.

The other reference is in JOHN 11:5, and it has to do with the home of three of Jesus' closest friends. We are told here that "Jesus loved Martha, and her sister, and Lazarus." Judging by what happened in that home. I think it was equally true that Martha, Mary, and Lazarus loved Jesus. *They had the kind of home to which He loved to come*. In spite of poor Martha's fussiness and her concern with food and meals (somebody has to be concerned with that!), there was an atmosphere that cordially welcomed the presence of the Son of God, and that gave him the rest and re-creation He so often needed.

I want that kind of home. I want everyone and everything within its walls to cry "Welcome!" to God and the Master. I want everyone within it to be a Martha, doing every chore from washing the dishes to kneeling in God's corner, in the knowledge that they do it to prepare the house for the coming of God. I want everyone in it to be a Mary, ready to sit at His feet when He comes, and learn from Him. I want everyone in it to be as quietly faithful, even unto death, as Lazarus was. I want a home in which every occupant will know that God is in it, every hour, every minute, and that He likes to be there.

There is a story—if it isn't true, it should be—about an American governor on one of the islands of the sea who said to the puzzled natives, "I'll have a democracy here, if I have to kill every one of you to get it!" We respect his admiration for democracy, but . . . ! He is too much like the parent who tried to spank his children into the Kingdom of God, saying to them, "You'll get religion, or else!" I like much better those parents and those homes in which love rules, even among the pots and pans.

7

What Is a Boy?

YOU MAY HAVE heard or read this; if you have, just skip it. But it is too good to leave out of this book, which has a lot to do with boys and girls. I pass these next two chapters on to you for what they may be worth to you. I am indebted to Alan Beck, who is listed as author of both "What Is a Boy?" and "What Is a Girl?" Anyone who knows a little boy or little girl may recognize them here.

"What is a boy?

"Between the innocence of babyhood and the dignity of manhood we find a delightful creature called a boy. Boys come in assorted sizes, weights and colors, but all boys have the same creed: to enjoy every second of every minute of every hour of every day, and to protest with noise (their only weapon) when their last minute is finished and the adult males pack them off to bed at night.

"Boys are found everywhere—on top of, underneath, inside of, climbing on, swinging from, running around, or jumping to. Mothers love them, little girls hate them, older sisters and brothers tolerate them, adults ignore them, and Heaven protects them.

"A boy is Truth with dirt on its face, Beauty with a cut on its finger, Wisdom with bubble gum in its hair, and the Hope of the future with a frog in its pocket.

"When you are busy, a boy is an inconsiderate, bothersome, intruding jungle of noise. When you want him to make a good impression, his brain turns to jelly or else he becomes a savage, sadistic jungle creature bent on destroying the world, and himself with it.

"A boy is a composite—he has the appetite of a horse, the digestion of a sword-swallower, the energy of a pocket-size atomic bomb, the curiosity of a cat, the lungs of a dictator, the imagination of a Paul Bunyan, the shyness of a violet, the audacity of a steel trap, the enthusiasm of a fire-cracker, and when he makes something he has five thumbs on each hand.

"He likes ice cream, knives, saws, Christmas, comic books, the boy across the street, woods, water (in its native habitat), large animals, trains, Saturday mornings, and fire engines.

"He is not much for Sunday school, company, schools, books without pictures, music lessons, neckties, barbers, girls, overcoats, adults, or bedtime.

"Nobody else gets so much fun out of trees, dogs, and breezes. Nobody else can cram into one pocket a rusty knife, a half-eaten apple, 3 feet of string, 2 gumdrops, 6 cents, a slingshot, a chunk of unknown substance, and a genuine supersonic code ring with a secret compartment.

"A boy is a magical creature—you can lock him out of your workshop, but you can't lock him out of your heart. You can get him out of your study, but you can't get him out of your mind.

"You might as well give up. He is your captor, your

jailer, your boss, and your master—a freckle-faced, pint-sized, cat-chasing bundle of noise. But when your dreams tumble down and the world is a mess, he can put together the broken pieces in just a twinkling, with a few magic words . . . 'I love you.' "

8

What Is a Girl?

"*LITTLE GIRLS ARE* the nicest things that happen to people. They are born with a little bit of angel-shine about them and though it wears thin sometimes, there is always enough left to lasso your heart—even when they are sitting in the mud, or crying temperamental tears, or parading up the street in mother's best clothes.

"A little girl can be sweeter (and badder) oftener than anyone else in the world. She can jitter around, and stomp, and make funny noises that frazzle your nerves, yet just when you open your mouth, she stands there, demure, with that special look in her eyes.

"A girl is Innocence playing in the mud, Beauty standing on its head, and Motherhood dragging a doll by the foot.

"Girls are available in five colors—black, white, red, yellow or brown, yet Mother Nature always manages to select your favorite color when you place your order. They disprove the law of supply and demand—there are millions of little girls, but each is as precious as rubies.

"God borrows from many creatures to make a girl. He uses the song of the bird, the squeal of a pig, the stubbornness of the mule, the antics of a monkey, the spryness of a grasshopper, the curiosity of a cat, the speed of a gazelle, the slyness of a fox, the softness of a kitten, and to top it all off He adds the mysterious mind of a woman.

"A little girl likes new shoes, party dresses, small animals, first grade, noise-makers, the girl next door, dolls, make-believe, dancing lessons, ice cream, coloring books, make-up, cans of water, going visiting, tea parties, and one boy.

"She doesn't care so much for visitors, boys in general, large dogs, hand-me-downs, straight chairs, vegetables, snow suits, or staying in the front yard. She is the loudest when you are thinking, the prettiest when she has provoked you, the busiest at bedtime, the quietest when you want to show her off, and the most flirtatious when she absolutely must not get the best of you again.

"Who else can cause you more grief, joy, irritation, satisfaction, embarrassment and genuine delight than this combination of Eve, Salome, and Florence Nightingale?

"She can muss up your home, your hair, and your dignity—then, just when your patience is ready to crack, her sunshine peeks through and you're lost again.

"Yes, she is a nerve-wracking nuisance, just a noisy bundle of mischief. But when your dreams tumble down and the world is a mess—when it seems you are pretty much of a fool after all—she can make you a king when she climbs on your knee and whispers, 'I love you best of all!' "

9
Prayer

INASMUCH AS WE are talking and thinking now about boys and girls, this may be a good time to take time out to talk about prayer and our children. You can't help thinking about it, if you read your newspapers or listen to radio and watch TV. It's a good time now to make up our minds about this business of prayer or no prayer in the public schools.

Yes, it's a tricky question. Every question that is important in our daily living and growing is tricky, and we have to allow for differences of opinion. We will have to admit, right at the start, that people, parents, educators, legislators hold different views on the outlawing of prayer in the schools.

I know—the Supreme Court decision, as some see it, did *not* outlaw prayer and the discussion of religion in the public school. At least, it did not intend to do that. All it did was to say that the *state* should not write or dictate the prayer, and force children of different religious persuasions to repeat it. That would be mixing "church and state," and the separation of church and state is a time-honored American and democratic principle. But the net result of it has been the banning of *all* prayer and religion from the schools, and I think this is a tragic mistake.

In the first place, I see no reason why one woman who is an atheist and who wants her children to grow up as atheists should be allowed to force her atheism upon all the rest of us who want our children to know and respect the name of God. I see no reason why a small minority of people in this country should be permitted to strike the "In God we trust" from our coins, or to take the name of God out of our pledge of allegiance to the flag, or to deny the boys in our armed services the presence of chaplains, or to stop the practice of opening sessions of Congress with prayer—and, believe it or not, *this is exactly what they want!* I don't get it! We lean over backwards in defending the rights of the minorities, and, being a democracy, we should. But what about the rights of the majority? Haven't they any rights to be protected? They call this freedom. Freedom for *whom,* and for *what?* I think it's time that all of us—particularly all of us parents—stood up and were counted on this question, lest we lose the very freedom under which, paradoxically, we allow these people to destroy the freedoms of others.

Jesus Christ said, ". . . ye shall know the truth, and the truth shall make you free" (JOHN 8:32). What's wrong with a child knowing His truth? He declared, "I am the way, the truth, and the life . . ." (JOHN 14:6). Why should a child be denied all the knowledge he can get about that Way and that life? Is it *sinful* to give him that? Jesus said, when He departed from the earth, He would send the Comforter, the Holy Spirit, to guide us into all truth. And how do we go about contacting this Holy Spirit, so that we may be guided to the truth? We do it through honest, constant, sincere prayer, in invoking the Spirit through communion with Him. We do it through the Guide Book we call the Bible—and we can never read enough or think enough about that Bible, in school or home or church or anywhere else. If the God of the Book becomes no longer our Supreme Authority in the affairs of men and nations, then what, or who, *is* the authority?

Are *people,* with all their confusions and conflicts and clashing opinions and differing interpretations, to be the final authority? Did you ever see two people who agreed on anything, down to the smallest detail? People must have a *standard* to live by if they want to live in peace, and not like beasts in the jungle. When a country goes off her economic standard, there is economic confusion. Right? When people desert their tried and tested moral standards, there is moral chaos. Right? And when we desert the religious standards that are warp and woof of our great country, and that have made us the great power we are in the family of nations—well, what then?

Are we to be governed by a minority which denies and rejects the moral and spiritual standards of this America, or by the majority which respects them? Are our children in the schoolroom to be penalized in being refused the privilege of even acknowledging the fact and presence of God, *wherever* they are? When prayer is offered in the public school, the child of the atheist is not compelled to repeat it; he is not even required to bow his head, not even required to attend such meetings in some schools. I see no "compulsion" in this.

But let me tell you something, ladies and mothers: there *is* compulsion in the opposite direction. These children of ours are too often a captive audience forced to listen to teachers and teaching that is agnostic and atheistic, and nobody seems to care a hoot about *that!* Many, many students are fed a slow, subtle diet of godless theology in our schoolrooms by dedicated doubters and atheists, and nobody objects. Why shouldn't a God-fearing, God-believing teacher be permitted to speak as freely?

I think it's true that the nonbelievers are still in the minority, among the teachers, but I think it's likewise true that they are on the increase, and that they are becoming really influential. The deadly poison of their thinking and writing, the preaching of their prophets, is sinking in. Take a good look at some of the books your children are required to read as "supplementary reading"; you will find many an author of the ungodly *avant-garde,* many a writer crying violently that the old moral standards are rubbish and should be thrown out on the scrap-heap as soon as possible. The worst of it is that, having thrown out the old standards, they offer no really decent new standards to take their place. The younger generation, or a great part of it, seems to me to be a generation without standards, and rebels against old causes with no new causes to fight for.

You think I am unduly alarmed? Just open your eyes and ears; read the papers—*carefully;* read the books your children are reading, particularly some of the science books and those in "social studies." Listen to the astounding and revolting declarations of some of our clergymen —often clergymen in high places—as they denounce as "out-moded" our time-tested and divinely-inspired rules of human behavior. Call me a square and old-fashioned if you want to, but I still tremble in fear for this younger generation when I read of a clergymen defending obscene books in court in the name of "freedom" and of one in particular who tried to distribute a disgusting, sex-packed biography as part of his "protest against censorship." Don't *we* dare protest against *anything*, any more?

Why do we have so much juvenile crime and delinquency? It's as plain as the nose on your face. Our children are given no moral or spiritual guidance in the school; family prayers have all but disappeared in the large majority of our homes, and many a child never enters a church or church school for the simple reason that their *parents* never enter them. When I went to school as a child in Osceola, Arkansas, we recited the Lord's Prayer in the classroom every morning, and on Fridays we had "chapel," with singing, Bible reading, prayer, and a minister from a different church to talk to us. I loved it, and all my schoolmates loved it; I have yet to hear of one of them saying it did him or her any harm. I was fortunate to have it like that—and fortunate to have the teaching continued in a home in which Bible-loving and churchgoing parents took up where the school left off. I pity the youngsters who do not have this today.

Do you remember what President Kennedy said, just after the Supreme Court decision? I cannot remember his exact words, but this was the gist of it: "All right. The Court has spoken. Now all of us must increase and deepen the teaching of religion, and cultivate the practice of prayer in our churches *and in our homes*." That's a pretty free translation of what he said, but that is its meaning, and he put his finger right on the heart of the problem that faces us now. Now the whole responsibility for spiritual nurture falls upon the shoulders of the church and the home. The school has some thirty-odd hours a week with our children, the church has three or four, the home has the rest—and we'd better make good use of them if we want an America that even approximates the status of a godly nation.

It's vital to our future and our freedoms. Mrs. Bela V. Dodd, a Christian lawyer, sat in a New York courtroom the day the news of the Supreme Court decision came through. Every lawyer in the room was excited about it, and talking about what it meant and would mean. One young lawyer, who seemed just out of law school, looked up at the motto on a placque behind the judge's bench— "In God We Trust"—and he said, "Good. That's the next thing to go." Mrs. Dodd was so stunned and repulsed by his words that she was silent for a moment; then she said, "Young man, I'm old enough to be your grandmother, and you can take my word for it: when that sign comes down, your career will be over, because there will be no real law for you to practice." Mrs. Dodd speaks out of bitter experience: as a former Communist she was once engaged in the anti-God crusade. She came back to God and common sense when she saw where that crusade was leading us.

Time out, ladies—for God, children, and country!

10

The Lord's Prayer

IF YOU ARE one of those people who do not pray much because you do not quite know *how* to pray, may I suggest that you start with a study of the most beautiful prayer in the world? All prayers are beautiful when they flow from the heart, but Jesus gave us this one, and it is the perfect model. Some students of the Bible say we shouldn't call it The Lord's Prayer, but the Disciple's Prayer, for Jesus gave it to His disciples to pray, and there is no evidence that He repeated it over and over as His own personal prayer. But it still stands, after all these years, as the noblest gem in the whole catalogue of prayer. I have read somewhere that "It has the delight of the familiar, and warms our hearts like an old song, an old house, an old church." Sir William Osler, the famous physician and philosopher, advises us: "Begin the day with Christ and His prayer—you will need no other. Creedless, with it you will have religion; creed-stuffed, it will leaven any theological dough in which you may stick."

Thank you, Dr. Osler! I am no theologian, and I often

get stuck in the confusing language of the theologians who speak a language I cannot always understand. But I can understand this prayer of Jesus in the sixth chapter of Matthew. It is so plain and so relevant to my problems that it burns like living fire!

Father Vincent McNab, an English clergyman, had a friend who knew the daughter of Karl Marx—who was no praying man, by any standard. He says that the two of them one day got to talking about religion, and the daughter of the father of Socialism said, "I was brought up without any religion. I do not believe in God." Then she added, wistfully, "But just the other day, in an old German book, I came across a German prayer, and if the God of that prayer exists, I think I could believe in Him." She didn't know the name of the prayer, or anything about its background, but she knew that it began with the words, "Our Father which art in heaven, Hallowed be they name. Thy kingdom come. Thy will be done in earth, as it is in heaven"—and that was enough. It is enough for me.

Let's see what it says.

Our Father which art in heaven. . . . That word "Father" brings Him close—as close as, or closer than, our earthly parents. He is Father of a family—the whole great human family—Father of *all* of us. The word breaks down barriers between us. We are all His creation, all potential sons and heirs of His Kingdom and love. That one word, Father, makes the world a brotherhood. Are you one of those who feel that "God is so far away . . ."? Or that He seems "so formal and cold"? That just isn't true! When you come to see God as a Father, there is a close, intimate relationship with Him.

Isn't it wonderful that God has allowed us to call Him that? With all His infinite greatness, He deigned to imbue us with His Holy Spirit? It is hard to fathom, but marvelous to contemplate. He said, through His Word and His prophets and His dedicated servants, that He is a Rewarder of them that seek Him diligently. I believe He wants us to constantly and consciously abide in His presence, and, even if silently, to talk with Him (pray!) through all our waking hours. My beloved son Tom once said to me that "pray without ceasing," to him, meant living one's life in an attitude of prayer. I have never forgotten that, and as I struggle in my pilgrimage, this is helpful advice to come back to from time to time.

Our Father which art in *heaven?* David Redding says that "This is God's world but not His home. His Kingdom has not yet come on earth as it is in heaven. We are not what we ought to be. So we point our spires toward the sky." Isn't that glorious? You can't confine God to this world; you can't fence Him in like that. *From heaven He rules the universe, and all that is within it.* He is Ruler of the universe—and He loves us and cares for us like a Father.

Dr. Armin C. Oldsen, who speaks over the Lutheran Hour broadcast, asks some pertinent questions about all this: "Is a good father strong? God is perfect strength. Is a good father wise? God is perfect wisdom. Is a good father loving? God is perfect love. Is a good father interested in the problems of his children? Does he take time to remove a stone from a little one's shoe? To apply a Band-aid, to fix a bicycle or doll, to help with the homework, to listen to troubles? If at all possible, he does. God, who is concerned about the business of running the universe, has time for the most trifling problems of those who are His children. A simple and sincere 'Our Father' will bring Him immediately to our side."

Where is heaven? Jesus said that the Kingdom of

heaven is within us. Again He said, ". . . the kingdom of heaven is at hand . . ." (MATTHEW 4:17)—all around us, close enough to touch, if one will just extend his heart. He said that God is a Spirit, and that we must worship Him in spirit and in truth—and, of course, He said, "I am . . . the truth . . ." (JOHN 14:6). The Spirit of God in its fullness was in Jesus. When He said that His Kingdom was not of this world, I believe He meant that His Kingdom was of the Spirit. When our souls are in tune with Almighty God, we feel rich indeed, and "on top of the world"—in *heaven*. When I accepted Jesus Christ as my personal Saviour, I truly experienced a new heaven and a new earth, for my darkened spirit was illumined, and my clay was washed in His powerful blood. I became a new creature in Him. This new creature is promised sustenance, for in Him I live and move and have my being. ". . . nevertheless I live; yet not I, but Christ liveth in me" (GALATIANS 2:20). In this experience, heaven has been brought to earth *for me*.

Hallowed be thy name. The opposite of hallowed is "profane"—and you cannot walk around the block these days without hearing someone, either consciously or unconsciously, profane the name of God. We are a blasphemous generation, and it must break the heart of God. It hurts Him and degrades us. Lord Byron said to a blasphemous friend that the friend was disgustingly blasphemous because he did not know what to say, and so he cursed to cover up his ignorance. Refusal to reverence, or "hallow," the name of God is a sign of stupidity, and it is unworthy of anyone who believes in God. Gipsy Smith once heard a pretty young girl take the name of God in vain; in that gentle way of his he said to her, "My dear, those pretty lips of yours were not made to take the name of the Lord in vain."

And "hallowing" means more than just *speaking;* we are guilty of blasphemy when we give God a divided allegiance; when we hold Him in disrespect; when we refuse to hold in high regard any other child of God than ourselves! *All life must be hallowed, for God created it.* May my life hallow His name. When I have departed this vale of tears, may any remembrance of me be found in the compliment, "She was a Christian." As the mother of Our Lord said at the moment of Annunciation, "My soul doth magnify the Lord, And my spirit hath rejoiced in God my Saviour" (LUKE 1:46,47). Oh, Holy Spirit of the living God, guard my subconscious mind in my sleep from the evil influences residing in the powers of darkness, and in my waking moments put a sentinel before my heart and lips, that I may eschew evil thoughts and actions and words. May thy blessed Spirit renew me, that Thy will may be performed daily.

Thy Kingdom come. When? How? Some of us seem to be praying, "Thy Kingdom come—but not just yet! I have some things to do, and do *my* way, before it comes!" Or, "Thy Kingdom *not* come, *my* will be done!" Let's get it straight. God's Kingdom is absolute. There is none other beside God. When we sing "My country, 'tis of Thee," the most marvelous part of the song, to me, is that which says, "Protect us by Thy might, great God, our King." Who can question His Kingship, or prevent the coming of His Kingdom? Through Him the Word, through the only begotten Son of the everlasting Father God was everything created; when He beheld His creation, He said it was good. We spoiled it for a time, but just as sure as he made little green apples this world one day will be made perfect again and He will rule in perfection forever. When we consider that in that day the lion shall lie down with the lamb—well, that will be truly heaven, will it not? No more tears, no more sickness, no more death, no more separation, hunger or thirst. That will be the Kingdom "come."

Thy will be done. . . . We'd better accept it: His will certainly *will* be done, whatever *we* do. God has the last word on earth and in heaven. When Lucifer and his unholy band of angels dared challenge the sovereignty of God, they were banished from heaven.

God also has the last word on the earth today. In the natural world we see natural law transcended by His Spirit. His will is done.

We have a good Christian friend who is a living example of God's power over the ravages of so-called incurable cancer. According to the doctors this man should have succumbed long ago to the "natural causes" inherent in such sickness, but he has not succumbed. He has a great faith in the God who rules all nature, and with the people who have been praying for him he is saying with God, "The time is not yet." Obviously, there is still work for him to do, and he is faithful in doing it as he goes on in the supreme confidence that it is all according to the will of God.

How can we know the mind and will of God? How can we know His plan for our daily lives? Deciding about that is most difficult, as all important decisions are difficult. It seems to me that the older I grow, the more difficult it becomes; the more I know, the more reluctant I am to accept responsibility for my decisions. When you face a major decision—like our friend's—well, how do *you* decide?

I think the best way to arrive at the right decision is to first pray about it, placing it in God's hands. Then sleep on it. The next morning, when you get up, I believe that the first solution that comes to your mind will be the right one—that is, if you have complete confidence in God's guidance. James has a good word of advice here: "But let him ask in faith, nothing wavering. For he that wavereth is like a wave of the sea driven with the wind and tossed" (JAMES 1:6). Ask God's help in faith, and your decision will be right. I have found it unwise to make important decisions at the end of the day, when we are weary and tired. But once we have made a decision, we must not look back, like Lot's wife. We must act then on the faith that God has given us the answer—and know that only good will come out of it.

Give us this day our daily bread. Notice that God does not say "tomorrow's bread." We are not to be concerned about tomorrow—only about today. A friend sent me this verse from the famous old hymn as a wall motto; I keep it above my kitchen sink:

Lord, for tomorrow and its needs I do not pray;
Keep me, my God, from stain of sin, just for today.
Now, set a seal upon my lips; for this I pray.
Keep me from wrong or idle words, just for today.
Let me be slow to do my will, prompt to obey,
And keep me, guide me, use me, Lord, just for today.

Below the poem are the words, "I will strengthen thee, yea, I will help thee," from ISAIAH 41:10.

What is bread? In the deepest sense, bread is Jesus Christ. Bread is sustenance. Jesus sustains us. He is our Manna, our Water of Life. ". . .whosoever drinketh of the water that I shall give him shall never thirst . . ." (JOHN 4:14). He satisfies every longing. If we seek first the Kingdom of God and His righteousness, all the things we *need* (not necessarily all the things we *want*) will be added unto us. He promised it, and He never breaks a promise. Bread! Our bodies can fast awhile and deny themselves bread, with no ill effect, but when the soul goes on a fast, look out! We need the bread of Christ in our souls every day.

And forgive us our debts, as we forgive our debtors. This is tremendously important; Jesus says that unless we forgive others, we cannot expect God to forgive us. It's a *must.* And it means something more than debts in money. Matthew uses the word "debts"; Luke says, "Forgive us our *sins"; some of us say "trespasses," as the Episcopal *Book of Common Prayer* and the Coverdale translation have it, but all three words count up to the same thing. The meaning is that any harm or wrong or sin should be forgotten and forgiven. We have all sinned; we have all done mean things to other people, and others have done mean things to us; we all hold grudges; we all have a sense of guilt in our souls for all this, whether we admit it or not. If we are to be rid of that load of guilt, we *must* forgive—and forget. A man said once to John Wesley, "I can never forgive the man who did this injury to me." And Wesley replied, "Then, my brother, I hope that you will never sin, since if you sin you will stand in need of the divine forgiveness."

The thing to remember is that the divine forgiveness does come when we learn to forgive others. "As far as the east is from the west, so far hath he removed our transgressions from us" (PSALMS 103:12). The Psalmist of the Old Testament believed that, Jesus believed it, and I believe it with all my heart and mind and soul. In Micah (7:19) we are promised that God will bury our sins in

70

the depths of the seas, and hold them against us no more. Jesus went to the cross that we might have this blessed forgiveness. To me, this is the greatest of the promises of God.

So we had better forgive others. If we keep the old grudge alive, if we go on rattling the old skeleton bones, we offer an insult to Christ's atonement for us. In that atonement He offered forgiveness for any and every sin we may commit—and yet, some folks seem to think that they are so high and mighty that they can commit a sin which His grace cannot cover, and bury. What audacity!

Let's remember this, too: we haven't really forgiven until we have forgotten. Ouch! That's hard to take, but it is true. Our big problem is pride: usually we can't forget a wrong done to us because our pride has been wounded and keeps smarting. But our pride needs to be wounded, mortally wounded, for our Lord *despises* pride. Remember what He said about the publican and the Pharisee praying in the temple? (Read it again, in LUKE 18.) I doubt that the Lord ever hears a prayer spoken in pride.

And lead us not into temptation. . . . I don't believe that the Lord leads us into temptation; I *do* believe James (1:13), in the Bible, when he says, ". . . for God cannot be tempted with evil, neither tempteth he any man." I do believe that God allows Satan to tempt us, and for a good purpose. Satan is the one who tries constantly to lead us astray, and he is cunning about it. He can rationalize sin until it seems to be "the natural thing to do." But "doing what comes naturally" is not doing what God would have us do. I think it is reasonable to think that Christ means here, "Protect us from *yielding* to temptation. . . ." God allows us to be tempted as a test of our strength in refusing to yield to the temptation. And only God can give us the strength to keep from yielding.

He is ready and willing to deliver us from evil, if we want to be delivered. But we can't be like the bird gazing at the cobra, allowing ourselves to be hypnotized and overcome. We must turn away from it, must seek that divine strength in overcoming it. We must remember that "God is our refuge and strength, a very present help in trouble" (PSALMS 46:1). Temptation is trouble—one trouble in which we *really* need God!

For thine is the kingdom. . . . It is interesting that these words were first spoken by King David, in I CHRONICLES 29:11: "Thine, O Lord, is . . . the power, and the glory, . . . thine is the kingdom, . . . and thou art exalted as head above all." David had quite an interest in kingdoms; he built a good one of his own—but he knew it was a trifling kingdom compared with God's. "The earth is the Lord's, and the fulness thereof . . ." (PSALMS 24:1). All of it belongs to Him; He has complete and final dominion. "He holds the whole world in His hands"—how I love that old spiritual! He holds the earth, the other planets and stars, He holds space in His hands. It is almost beyond comprehension, to me, and I am glad it is. Where would be the awe, the mystery, and the majesty of the great ultimate power behind the universe if we could completely understand this great God of ours? If I could completely understand Him, I might get tired of Him. Why do people want to put God in a test tube? I don't. I cannot. There just isn't a test tube big enough.

. . . *the power and the glory.* . . . Power! Imagine the Power that created the whole universe! Go out at night and just look up at the stars, at the countless galaxies swinging in the sky, and you will *feel* that power! Only

72

God could have thought of it, only God could have done it. We poor, insignificant human beings think that if we can only land someone on the moon we shall at last have dug out another of the secrets of God—so, after all, He isn't as important as human science! Listen, ladies: God is *all* of science. He is all-knowing, all-understanding, all-powerful—and all love.

Let us never forget that we are absolutely nothing without God. Said Jesus, ". . . without me, ye can do *nothing*" (JOHN 15:5). The daisy has nothing to do with being a daisy, with having white petals and a yellow center and a green stem. Yet, when the daisy blooms and turns her face to the sun, she glorifies God with her beauty. Let the beauty of Jesus be seen in us!

Dr. William L. Stidger used to tell a story about an old Negro boatman who worked hard at the monotonous, dirty job of running his little boat, and he sang all day long as he worked. Dr. Stidger asked him how he did it, and the old man replied, "Sir, I'se got a *glory*." It has happened to me. My life was changed from grime to glory when I turned to walk with God in Christ. I walk in the sun. I pray that you may, too.

11
Prayer for
the Middle-Aged

WHILE WE'RE ON the subject of prayer, let me say
this—and I hope it does not disturb you too much: I
think too many of us tend to become parrots in our
praying. That is, we find it so much easier to read prayers
written by someone else than to pray in our own
words and out of our own hearts. And that's an indica-
tion that we are lazy.

I think we should know The Lord's Prayer by heart,
and repeat it often; it is Christ's suggestion as to how we
should pray and, generally, for what. But I do not believe
that we should stop with that. We should grow in
prayer, with His prayer as a starting-point. Our prayers
should be concerned with life as it is, as it grows and
changes. It should be a two-way conversation with God
about the things that face us *now*.

I like that grace said at the table in the boarding-house,
in the play *You Can't Take It With You.* You may recall
it. The plain-spoken old man who ran the boarding-house
would stand up at the head of the table and he would
begin, as the boarders bowed their heads, "Well, Sir, here

we are again!" Or there was the little boy who used to go into his church all alone to pray; when the minister asked him how he prayed, and what he asked God for, he replied, "I don't ask Him for nothin'. I just say, 'Lord, it's Jimmie.'" Good for Jimmie! The Lord knows our needs, and He waits patiently for us to come to Him with them!

I thought about this when I ran across the following "Prayer for the Middle-Aged." It is such an arresting and unusual and heart-stirring prayer that I just have to pass it along to you. I'm not asking you to copy it, or to memorize it, but I think it might help if you could get some of its heartening frankness and honesty into your praying. Here it is:

"Lord, Thou knowest better than I know myself that I am growing older and will some day be old. Keep me from the fatal habit of thinking I must say something on every subject and on every occasion. Release me from craving to straighten out everybody's affairs. Make me thoughtful but not moody; make me helpful but not bossy. With my vast store of wisdom, it seems a pity not to use it at all, but Thou knowest, Lord, that I want a few friends at the end.

"Keep my mind free from the recital of endless details; give me wings to get to the point. Seal my lips on my aches and pains. . . . I dare not ask for grace enough to enjoy the tales of others' pains, but help me to endure them with patience.

"I dare not ask for improved memory, but for growing humility and a lessening cocksureness when my memory seems to clash with the memories of others. Teach me the glorious lesson that occasionally I may be mistaken.

"Keep me reasonably sweet: I do not want to be a saint. A sour old person is one of the crowning works of the devil. Give me the ability to see good things in unexpected places and talents in unexpected people. Give me the grace to tell them so. . . . Amen."

Source unknown

Like it?

12

About Clothes, and Growing Gracefully

TODAY, LET'S TALK about clothes and growing up—and old.

I plead guilty to needing that prayer for the middle-aged, for I am no longer a sweet sixteen, even though I am not conscious of any great ravages wrought upon me by the passing years. I still feel young, and the years don't matter.

So many women and girls have asked me what I do to "look so young," what I do to "keep going"; at my age, they want to know what the secret is. Well, there's nothing mysterious about it. It's as Stuart Hamblen puts it in his hit song, "It Is No Secret, What God Can Do!" The credit doesn't belong to me at all; it belongs to God. Since I accepted the Lord Jesus as Saviour and Lord of my life, and asked Him to work through me, the responsibility for my staying young was upon Him, for I became the instrument through which He worked His Way, and His Way is the Way of the eternally young in spirit.

Once I had done that, I found that of myself I could

accomplish nothing really worthwhile, but that anything was possible when I gave Jesus the reins. Jesus said that if we have faith as a grain of mustard seed, then " . . . nothing shall be impossible unto you" (MATTHEW 17:20). It is as simple as that.

I do try, by His Grace, to take care of my body and my mind; I think this is a large part of His plan for me. The Bible says that our bodies are the temples of His Holy Spirit. It is, therefore, our responsibility to take care of those bodies so that He can work better through us. I do not dissipate with late hours, alcohol, tobacco, overeating, or intemperance in *anything*. I watch my weight and I exercise every day. I eat lots of raw vegetables (what I can eat raw, I rarely cook), lots of fresh and stewed fruits, skimmed milk and yogurt and buttermilk, eggs and lean meat, and I try to get plenty of sleep. I read a lot—Scripture, devotional books, and the newspapers— to see what is going on in the world. Sometimes what I read is pretty discouraging, but when I read in my Bible that Jesus said, "Heaven and earth shall pass away, but my words shall not pass away" (MATTHEW 24:35), I take heart again, and know that His hand is upon us all. Since He is the Word, we can depend upon Him, no matter what the world does! I do lots of praying; I couldn't live without prayer. I pray at home and in the street and in my car—I do a lot of praying in the car, since I live out in the country and spend a lot of time traveling. It's great, praying in a car—just sentence prayers, or meditative praise, just looking at God's wonderful world and thanking Him for it, and for His care.

Of course, I try to look my best. I think a Christian woman is obligated to look her best and to do the best she can with what the Lord gave her. A minister said once, as he passed a woman on the street who wore the ugliest possible clothes and no make-up at all, "We're ugly enough as it is, without adding anything to it!" And I think it was Billy Graham (forgive me, Billy, if it wasn't you) who said to a lady who asked him if women should wear make-up, "If it helps her to look better, I think it's all right for a woman to use some—and *you* could use some!" I know—there are some perfectly sincere Christians who think it is somehow sinful for a woman to wear make-up or jewelry. That's their opinion, and I respect it. If I thought it were a sin to wear make-up or jewelry, or to "rat" my hair, then for me to do it would be wrong, and my heart would tell me so. But my heart just doesn't say so. I wear jewelry and use make-up when I feel like it, and I have even been known to wear a wig. For, you see, so many young people remember me in western pictures, and they have an "image" of me, and I feel that they would feel let down if I were to appear without make-up.

But let me keep it clear that I believe the chief adornment of the Christian woman is the adornment of the Spirit of God glowing on her face and in her eyes. This is always breathtakingly beautiful to me, and you can never miss it, whether a woman wears jewelry or lipstick, or not. Any woman looks somehow colorless without that Spirit lighting her countenance; it's what's inside that counts.

Whenever this subject comes up, I think of what Miss Henrietta Mears said once. Henrietta Mears was one of the finest Christian women I have ever known—and you will find literally thousands of others who will tell you the same thing. Now Miss Mears was given to jewelry, big hats, party dresses—all of which she wore to the glory of God. A well-meaning Christian gentleman once told her that she offended him by her mode of dress, and that a Christian woman of her stature should be more "subdued." She looked him straight in the eye, reached out and pulled out his necktie and stood looking at it; then in her devastating way she asked him, "Young man, why do you wear that bright tie?" 'Nuff said! What a woman! What a Christian!

The good Lord in His wisdom gave us the songs of the birds; He expected us to enjoy them. He gave us love; He expects us to enjoy it. Don't you think so? I believe that the birds sing His praises, and I believe that a well-dressed woman or girl does the same thing, with the Spirit of Christ in her heart; she is "wondrous to behold." They make good "fisherwomen," too, when it comes to recruiting souls for the Lord. I know some lovely ones, and it thrills me to see them and hear them talk of their experiences with the Lord. I think God meant them to be just like that. Jesus never told Mary Magdalene—or any other woman (at least, I've never seen it in the Bible)—to change her manner of dress or the way she wore her hair. He said, ". . . go, and sin no more" (JOHN 8:11).

Of course, there's a limit. The Bible is severe in its judgment upon over-painted women. Jezebel, looking out from her overdone face, is a repulsive woman. Some of us have outdone Jezebel, and are doing something even she never dared to do: we have invented the topless bathing suit, and the topless cocktail dress, and I am told that some women are even wearing them (when they can avoid the police!)—and in some places, the law upholds their disgraceful attire! Well, I never! Isn't anything sacred, any more?

I know. These women say, "Well, the men don't have to look!" Oh, no? Who are they kidding? Other women are saying that "We women deserve more respect than the men are giving us." Maybe so—but do we get it this way?

Let's be honest: what is the motive for this undressing? What's in the mind of our "modern daughter of Eve"? Is she honest when she says she goes for this nudity because it gives her "charm" in the eyes of men? She may be honest if she thinks that, but she's about as stupid as they come. There are two things I want to say about this nudity business, and the first is this: women (especially once they've passed twenty-five) will be smart if they do *not* unveil their "heavenly" charms. A woman is far more alluring when her curves are covered—and any honest woman knows it, and most men seem to think so. Talk with any man who has traveled in the South Sea Islands, where women wear as little as possible, and you'll find that their ultimate reaction is a big disgusted "ugh!" Displaying the curves doesn't charm anybody; it usually makes people laugh or look away.

If this is for the benefit of the men (and I think it is, in the shallow mind of any woman who would go for it), then the women had better remember that the men like modesty and *mystery* in women. They like to be the pursuers, not the pursued; they are fascinated with what is hidden in a woman's mind and heart. Do you think Caesar and Anthony were lured by the undress of Cleopatra, or by the queenly dignity and the inscrutable mystery of those black Egyptian eyes?

These modern topless (and brainless and moral-less) women are more brazen and godless—and dumb—than Cleopatra ever was. They are getting so brazenly godless that they think they are somehow like Diana the goddess. We're far out, girls. Clean gone. If we really want to "charm," we'd better get back to the old niceties of womanhood that provided a little cushioning for the harsh realities of life. Is this mid-Victorian reasoning? If it is, make the most of it! I like it better than the twentieth-century shock-treatment we women are giving out to the poor, out-numbered and helpless men who start laughing once the initial shock has registered. I believe women were happier when they observed the time-honored proprieties. There was a security in that which we do not have now.

All right, call me a square if you want to. I've been called that, and a lot worse, and I don't mind it a bit. As a matter of fact, I like that word "square," and I think it was and still is a very good and worthy word in its original meaning. To be square means to be honest with myself and with others. It has the meaning of the old song we used to sing, "I'd Rather Be Right Than President." I still think it is better to be decently honest than to imitate the girl who is so "show-business-conscious" that she calls in the photographers for her horseless Lady Godiva debut. I think she's a nut—and, if you don't mind the pun, she's riding for a fall.

And I like the old-fashioned Biblical approach to the human body. The Bible calls the body "the temple of the Holy Ghost," and I just haven't any respect for any human being who will blaspheme and outrage this or any other temple.

13
Race

I AM ABOUT to stick my foot in a hornet's nest—but here goes! I'd like to talk a little about race, inasmuch as everybody else in the United States is talking about it. None of us can avoid it, and none of us should, for the sake of our children. It's a revolution, and our youngsters will be involved in it wherever they are, whether they want to be involved or not.

It is especially difficult for me to discuss it, thanks to my background. I am the daughter of a Mississippi father and a Texas mother. My father was one of the finest men I have ever known, and a gentleman of the old Southern tradition and ideology. His father, my grandfather, owned a large "mercantile store" and some good land. When my Dad was born, my grandmother's health was bad, so my father had a wonderfully lovable Negro mammy who nursed him and loved him as her own. And he loved her. Her parents had been slaves in the family, and she was just a little girl when they were freed, and they didn't want freedom at all if it meant leaving our family—the only family they had known. There was love in that household.

Granddad was a fine Christian man—and he believed in segregation. He had been raised that way, and his father before him. The Negroes in their household had always been regarded as children who were supposed to serve and, in turn, be fed and housed and cared for—and shown affection. But they were never treated as social equals. My mother, being a Texan, had never had so many Negroes around her home as my father, but she, too, had been raised to believe that Negroes had their place, and that we had ours.

From the time I was a child, this never really "jelled" with me. I couldn't understand it. I had been raised in this tradition, but when I was in lower grade school I had the temerity to challenge my father on the matter. We were operating a cotton farm at the time, out in the country. We had a Negro family living on the farm, working for us. They had children about the same age as my brother and I. My brother and I had a lot of fun playing with those children, but as soon as company came we were told that we must not be seen playing with the Negro children. I protested to my father and he said, "Hush, child! You don't know what you are talking about." It bothered me.

To my knowledge, I have never been discourteous to a Negro, or to any other person of a different race than mine. I think, if we ever get this thing settled, that we will have to be a lot more courteous and understanding than we are now. I think we will have to put up a better demonstration of Christian love for each other, and I am sure in my heart that only a genuine spirit of Christian love will solve our race problem. I do not know why God made some people brown, and some black, yellow, red, or white, and it's not for me to question Him, but to be glad for the variety he has given us in humanity. What a dull world this would be if we were all exactly alike! But, mind you, He has made the same moon and the same seasons for all of us. The blood runs red in all of us. The same Spirit is in all of us. We are *all* living souls for whom Christ died.

I also believe that in our free America everyone should enjoy an equality of opportunity. Every person who lives decently and works hard should be allowed to attain his goal, regardless of race, creed, or color. I certainly believe that every citizen who is of proper age, who can read and write and carry out the duties of citizenship, should be allowed to vote, for American government is representative of all the people, and they should all be represented in the government.

I do not believe that *social* acceptance can be legislated or enforced by law. All of us must *earn* acceptance, respect, and friendship. It is a difficult process. Some people just don't take to other people, even within the same race. But I think they should have the same chance to live well. I think it was Bishop Paul Hardin of the Methodist Church who tells of how he played as a young white boy in the South with a colored boy. Both, in their first childhood aspirations, wanted to be engineers on the big locomotives that ran through their town. The Bishop, as a grown man, got the chance to sit in a locomotive cab and run the engine down the track past the very place where he and colored Jim used to watch the big iron monsters go by, and he says he had a strange thought as he sat there with his hand on the throttle. He said he realized that *he* could be an engineer, if he wanted to—but that Jim could not, for the simple ghastly reason that Jim happened to be black and not white. See what I mean? I think that wrong, and unchristian—and so does Bishop Hardin.

Why are we so fearful today of races other than our own, and so distrustful of people of those other races? Is it because we are lacking in that real faith in God which inspires love and trust in and concern for our neighbors? I think so. Our missionaries are successful with people of other races when they demonstrate their sincerity in loving those people; the natives can sense their sincerity, and they respond accordingly. The opposite is also true. Hate people and they will hate you; fasten a chain around the neck of a fellow man, and the other end will fasten itself around *your* neck. Love—God's love—never fails. It may take a little time, but love will win, for love is constructive in its compassion: it lifts!

We are all brothers and sisters in Christ; through Him, we are all the adopted children of God. This may sound involved, but I believe it. We are often called "an international family," and I see nothing strange or impossible about that. Wasn't the world made by one Father? (This reminds me of the southern mountain woman who heard the rumbling echoes of an atomic bomb explosion. She came rushing in to her husband, crying, "Paw, God's destroyin' the world!" The husband said quietly, "Well, it's His'n, ain't it?") The Bible tells us God ". . . hath made of one blood all nations of men for to dwell on all the face of the earth, and hath determined . . . the bounds of their habitation" (ACTS 17:26).

Now, some Bible scholars tell me that the general idea of this drawing of boundary or territorial lines by the Almighty was that each nation, assigned its territory, was supposed to stay within those boundary lines—that they were not supposed to mix or marry with anyone on the other side of the line. Maybe so. I'm not arguing with them, but it does seem to me that there was a lot of mixing and marrying in the ancient days, by all nations and all peoples. The Jews "crossed" into Canaan—remember? Territorial limits never seemed to mean very much to them, either then or now; they have moved into every nation on the face of the earth. How do we know who married whom, away back there in early Jewish history, before marriage records were filed at City Hall?

Jesus put it on higher, better ground; while the Jews were hating the Samaritans, He sat with a Samaritan woman at a well, and He made a deathless hero of a "Good Samaritan." He laughed at boundaries when He said that we should love the Lord our God (who had made of one blood all nations of men) *and* our neighbors as ourselves. It was the quality and presence of the Holy Spirit in the human heart. His arms were stretched wide on the cross—wide enough to hold *all* men, be they Jews or Romans or what have you.

Don't mistake me, and don't you dare misquote me! I am not advocating intermarriage of the races, for two reasons. One is that few such marriages are successful; the other is that the penalty of social ostracism falls not so much upon the mothers and fathers in these marriages, as it often does upon their innocent children. It is a high price to pay—and it is a price still paid even in most regions of the world.

I believe that only the true practice of God's love can settle this problem. We whites must extend ourselves in understanding helpfulness to our colored brothers and sisters. They can learn from us and we can learn from them. They could use some of our sense of responsibility, and we could certainly make good use of their art of relaxation and joy in simple pleasures. They have a marvelous trust in God—a simple, all-out faith that we should study and not ridicule. They have a singing religion—and religion should be a singing affair for all of us, whatever our color or creed.

Several years ago, in Los Angeles, I enjoyed speaking in an interracial church. The choir was solidly Negro, and could they sing! I wanted to shout "Hallelujah!" all over the place. There were also Chinese, Japanese, and Caucasian people in the congregation. Each racial group had its own missionary circle and project. Once a month they had a big "whing-ding" of a dinner in which everybody participated in cooking the food and arranging the program. Marvelous! What Spirit I felt there! That church is a living testimony to the presence of God's grace in interracial relations.

I have thought since that Christ would have enjoyed coming to that service. But no—He *was* there!

14
Gossip

LET'S FACE IT, ladies: one of the meanest of our feminine sins is gossip. Don't you love it? Some of my best friends are Grade-A gossips, and there are times when I am just as good at it as they are. I hate myself afterwards, but it just seems to be built-in with most of us. (Maybe it is with the men, too; I have known some men who could beat any Grade-A female without half trying. It is a sin not exclusive with the women.)

Someone gave Roy a motto for his desk; there was no ulterior motive in it, or any subtle suggestion that the lord of our manor was talking too much; I think it is a part of the Optimist Creed; it reads:

> Is it the truth?
> Will it hurt anyone?
> Will it help anyone?

There's more, but this is enough to start anyone thinking about gossip. It is really good advice, too, but who can remember it every time we get together, and a juicy little bit of sub rosa news pops up? Most of us would forget such advice then, for at such moments—the moments in which gossip is born—we tend to become malicious. We may not admit it, and we may claim that a little good gossip never hurt anybody, but I think most of it is done with malicious intent. Sometimes we gossip about others to salve our own consciences, and sort of pat ourselves on the back and say, "I'm not so bad, after all. Look at what *she* did!" How malicious can we get?

Gossip has ruined many careers, many churches, many marriages, many lives—especially where we live.

When you are married in Hollywood, and if you are in the news or "hot with the public press," you can, if you don't watch it, find yourself forced into a whirlpool of rumor, doubt, and distrust that lasts from morning to night, and all through the night. You who live in Philadelphia or Podunk or New York or almost anywhere else between Boston and Los Angeles can see a married man flirt with another man's wife at the country club on Saturday night, and you may hear a few remarks about it, but by the time Monday morning rolls around you've pretty much forgotten it. Not so in Hollywood! Out here it is built up and blown up and enlarged and magnified until it is a really big thing, known from coast to coast. Those involved in it at first try to laugh it off; if that doesn't work and the rumor persists, somebody a hundred miles away will begin to think that "Where there's smoke, there's fire," and by the time it makes the magazines and the newspapers, the injured party, to retain his or her pride, goes for a divorce. Many, many of these marriages could be saved *if only people would stop gossiping*.

No Christian man or woman has any business in the gossip business. If he does get into it, he hasn't any real concept of what Christianity means. My Bible tells me, in JAMES 1:26: "If any man among you seem to be religious, and bridleth not his tongue, but deceiveth his own heart, this man's religion is vain." What an indictment!

I know a fine woman in Fort Worth, Texas, who once belonged to a club in which the gossip was getting out of hand. When it came her turn to entertain, she bought a beautiful electric-lighted picture of the Last Supper, and hung it in a conspicuous spot in her living room. It worked quite a miracle. Whenever one of the gossipers was about to wind up and let go with a choice morsel of local scandal, she would look up and see that picture— and change the subject. It might help all of us, in many ways, to have such a picture in our house. I know it's a good thing to have a Bible close at hand, or a Bible verse hanging on the wall; they serve as gentle reminders that "whatsoever things are true, whatsoever things are honest, whatsoever things are just, whatsoever things are pure, whatsoever things are lovely, whatsoever things are of good report; if there be any virtue, and if there be any praise, think on these things" (PHILIPPIANS 4:8).

Think *hard*. Is what you are about to say true, just, pure, honest, lovely, a good *report?* If it isn't, don't say it. Here's a good rule for your dining-room table: "If you can't say anything good about a person, don't say anything at all." Then you won't want to cut out your tongue after the meal is over!

15

Church

WHAT IS CHURCH? Do you belong to a church? If so, do you attend regularly, or spasmodically? Are you one of those who say you can worship God without attending or helping to support the church?

Personally, I do not believe that simply joining a church will save anybody's soul for now and eternity. I believe we must have a personal, spiritual encounter with the Lord Jesus Christ and accept Him as Saviour and Lord of our lives; and that we are required by His grace to follow His teachings to the best of our ability.

The church, to me, is that great body of believers in the humanity and divinity of Jesus Christ; His sinless human life; His vicarious atonement for us on the cross of Calvary; His bodily resurrection from the tomb and His appearing to His followers afterwards; His ascension into heaven and His place at the right hand of God the Father Almighty, where he continually pleads the cases of His erring, but striving-to-please, children. Yes, I'm one of those old-fashioned Christians who believes that Mary, the mother of our Lord, was a virgin, and that He was conceived in her by the Holy Ghost. Why should anything not be possible with God? My God is too big for me even to attempt to measure.

95

I like a church that believes this. I cannot conceive of God having limited creativity and power. What a field day old Satan is having these days, with this one and that one saying that God is dead (regardless of how they mean it, it's dangerous when it's broadcast on a national TV network to a country that was founded on belief in God), and that Jesus wasn't really divine (so say some distinguished clerics and theologians), but was just a man who had more divinity than any other man.

If we have to understand every single spiritual thing with our puny brains, then there is no place or use for faith at all! Just because God hasn't been seen in outer space doesn't mean that God is not real. How many people can see an atom with the naked eye? God's there, all right, and He's here, inside you and me; if we will accept Him in simple faith, we will realize His presence.

Jesus said, "Except ye be converted; and become as little children, ye shall not enter into the kingdom of heaven" (MATTHEW 18:3). How dare we "shoot out the lip" at God with our human and intellectual speculations that change from year to year? Whatever and wherever heaven is, I'm on my way to it, and I am satisfied that the Bible is a dependable book of instruction on how to steer my course.

I agree with St. Paul that we should not forsake the practise of assembling together in corporate worship, for therein lies warm fellowship, and hope for our walk toward our desired haven, which is everlasting peace with Him who knew no sin, but became sin for us, that through His blood we might be reconciled to God.

Our son Dusty has just finished a film for Youth for Christ entitled *To Forgive a Thief*. He is appearing at youth rallies where the film is shown and giving his personal Christian testimony. In Barstow, California, he and Bob Turnbull (an actor who actively participates in the Hollywood Christian group and who also appeared in the film) were telling of their Christian experiences. Bob, who has a good sense of humor, prefaced his talk with "You know, folks, in heaven there isn't going to be a single Baptist!" He said this in a Baptist church. Needless to say, his remark caused a considerable stir. Then he added "There won't be any Methodists either, or Presbyterians, Lutherans, Nazarenes, Catholics—there will just be Christians." I go along with him on that. No denomination card will be a magical "open sesame" at the gates of pearl. I believe that the admitting angel will look for a brand stamped in the blood of Christ as the qualification to enter the heavenly portals.

We have belonged to many churches since we came to the Lord in 1948. I surrendered my life to Him in the Fountain Avenue Baptist Church in Hollywood. I had already accepted Him as Saviour in the First Baptist Church of Osceola, Arkansas, at age ten, and was baptized by immersion at that time. Roy was baptized three weeks after he accepted Christ, shortly before Easter, 1948, also at the Fountain Avenue Baptist Church. Our son Tom accepted Christ in full commitment at the age of ten in Italy, Texas, when he was staying with my parents during the time I was traveling with a band; he was baptized by immersion there, at the Central Baptist Church. Cheryl came to the Lord shortly after Roy and I did, and was immersed at Fountain Avenue Baptist Church.

Dusty was christened in the Little Brown Church in Studio City, California, at six months of age. He accepted Christ at seventeen and was baptized (at his request) by immersion at the Chapel in the Canyon in Canoga Park, California. Linda Lou was baptized and confirmed her faith in Jesus Christ in St. Nicholas Episcopal Church in Encino, California. John David ("Sandy," our adopted son who passed away in Germany on October 31, 1965) and Dodie were also christened at St. Nicholas Episcopal Church—Sandy at age five and Dodie at ten months. Sandy, Dodie, and Debbie—all three—gave their hearts to Christ at the Billy Graham Crusade in Los Angeles, when Billy was appearing at the coliseum there. Sandy asked to be immersed, and he was, along with Dusty, at the Chapel in the Canyon. Dodie so far has decided to rest on her christening at St. Nicholas. By the time this is published, Dodie probably will have been confirmed in her Christian faith in the Church of the Valley, Presbyterian, in Apple Valley, California, where we are now making our home.

Marion, our foster daughter from Scotland (who came to live with us at age twelve), was raised in a Church of Scotland orphanage in Edinburgh, Scotland; she confirmed her faith at St. Nicholas in Encino. Roy and I were also accepted and confirmed at St. Nicholas when we lived in Encino. At present, Roy and I are members at the Church of the Valley, Presbyterian, in Apple Valley. Dusty attends the High Desert Baptist Church in Victorville, where he is active in Youth for Christ work and sings in the choir. Debbie, our lovely Korean daughter who is now with the Lord, was baptized and received into the Chatsworth Methodist Church, Chatsworth, California, which our family joined when we first moved to Chatsworth.

So you see, we have belonged to, and been a part of, many different churches of Christian faith. We have attended and been blessed in many others. Wherever the

Gospel of Jesus Christ is preached, we feel at home, regardless of the name out front.

Christians in the church are the body of Christ. We are His earthly eyes, shoulders, arms, torso, legs, feet—Who can say which part is best? Do they not all make up the whole body?

Everything needed to guide us, as Christians, through this vale of tears, can be found in the Bible, God's Word. We believe that any assembly that calls itself Christian should faithfully present the Gospel in its entirety. Salvation, through Jesus Christ, is the very backbone of the Christian faith.

Yes, we believe in the church! My grandfather Wood advised his large family of seven daughters and one son, "When you move to a new place and want to make friends, go to the church, for there you will find the best people." I agree with him. They may not be perfect people (indeed, who is?), but most of them know that. That's why they go to church—for help to become better people and to grow in the knowledge and love of God.

16
Questions
About Sin

HI, LADIES! FEEL like discussing a subject this morning that most of us try to ignore or ridicule? Something we say we don't believe in too much, because nobody seems to know quite what it is?

I mean sin.

Don't tell me you don't believe in it, please! You do. Do you leave your car locked when you go to church? Are you glad there is a police force in your town? Do you put your money in a bank, behind a steel burglarproof door five feet thick, instead of just keeping it around the house? Do you spank your youngsters occasionally when they "do something they know they shouldn't do," or just because, somehow, "It's *wrong?*" Sure you do! Yes, you believe in sin, if your actions mean anything at all.

Some folks challenge me with the old question, "All right—just what is sin, anyway? Define it for me." That isn't very difficult. Sin is anything that keeps you from God. Sin is any thought or action that builds a wall between yourself and God. Sin is living by a low standard instead of a high one—we might say, by the devil's standard, instead of God's.

Some others side-step with the old crack that "Sin is *relative*, isn't it? What's sin to the African native isn't sin to the man in Hollywood or Hohokus." Oh, no? Stealing is sin the world over; just try it in the Congo! (I know all about the little tribe in India, in which stealing is a virtue, but they look pretty small and insignificant when we think of three billion people in the world.) Murder and lying and blasphemy are condemned everywhere. The *details* may differ, but the underlying principles are the same, and sin remains sin the world around. What do you mean, *relative?* James says, ". . . to him that knoweth to do good, and doeth it not, to him it is *sin*" (JAMES 4:17). Nothing relative about that, is there?

Sin carries a price tag. It costs. The price is high, and the product definitely not worth it. Sin is any transgression of God's law of love, and when we break that law—just as when we break any man-made law—we pay for it. Read the Ten Commandments and the declarations of Christ on sin; then find the opposite of these Commandments and declarations, and you have sin in proper focus.

Jesus recognized the fact that man, being formed in the flesh, is "sin prone"—that is, he is forever *liable* to sin. But we are supposed to try, by God's grace, to *avoid* sinning as much as is within us possible. He knew we would sin, because He alone is Perfection, and He gave us a picture of Perfection in His Sermon on the Mount. At best, we are but a poor reflection of that picture. This is why He atoned for our sin—because He was Perfection, and only Perfection could satisfy Perfection, in the divine justice.

A friend of mine once said to me, "I don't think God

102

can forgive me for all the things I have done in my life; I have done too much." That's an old one; it's like saying, "Oh, I'm human, after all, and so I just suppose I will go on sinning, and hope against hope that God will be merciful enough to forgive me, in the end—but I doubt it!" In my opinion, that statement is just as great a sin, and maybe worse, than fleshly, carnal sin, for it implies that God is not great enough or big enough to blot out every sin. If you say it, your God is not big enough. To me, God is God, and with Him all things are possible. Isaiah said, "Come now, and let us reason together, saith the Lord: though your sins be as scarlet, they shall be as white as snow . . ." (ISAIAH 1:18). That meant much in the Old Testament; how much more it means in the New, where we find Christ's blood washing away the scarlet of our sins! But we must ask Him to do it, and not just sit around waiting for Him to volunteer; we must make the effort to reach and know Him. He said, ". . . him that cometh to me I will in no wise cast out" (JOHN 6:37). He is alive, at the right hand of the Father in eternity, pleading for us and for the forgiveness of our sins, and sending the Holy Spirit with our spirit that we are forgiven.

Then there are those who ask me, "How can you get up and flay yourself for your sins in public, when you give your Christian witness?" They do not understand—or maybe they don't approve of public confession because they do not see its value. This is my reply to that question: "My life, including my personal pride, is hid with Christ, in God, in forgiveness. I believe it will help others to see what Christ can do with a life that is fully committed to Him. I was forgiven much; therefore I am very grateful, and I love Him much—and I am anxious that others find the same forgiveness and love." What He did for me, He can do for anyone. I do not "flay myself" to boast, but to win others.

Others ask, "What do you mean when you say you had an experience with the Lord—an *emotional* experience? I have accepted Christ as Lord, but I didn't experience any great emotional upheaval with it." Maybe so. The Spirit works in different ways with different people, and for me it was an experience packed with feeling, which is another name for emotion. I can't somehow think of conversion without feeling, any more than I can imagine a man proposing to a girl and a girl accepting the proposal without *some* fire under the boiler, if you get what I mean. Perhaps, if some people were as cold as ice when they experienced conversion, they were not carrying such a sense of guilt as I carried, and so they didn't feel such a sensation of relief as I felt. Perhaps they had little for which to be forgiven. I felt that I had a great deal.

To me, it's like a child who steals a cookie from the cookie jar, tells his mother about it, and is forgiven. It's a small sin, but at the moment of forgiveness he relaxes in a grateful smile and goes his merry way. But the same child, later, may steal a sum of money from his mother; this is a vastly greater sin, and he knows it, and if and when he has confessed that and found forgiveness again, the impact of the gesture of forgiveness is much more emotional, for the relief and the gratitude are that much greater.

We are inherently sinful because of our human natures; we have all sinned, and fallen short of the glory of God, and the Bible says that if we say we have no sin, we lie. Even the great Paul confessed to everlasting sin when he said that the things he would (should) do he did not, and the things he would (should) not do, he did. But he rejoiced—as we should rejoice—in the fact that God has furnished in Christ the remedy for sin. Like Paul, we have to ask for it when we fall—and fall we will, sooner or later, no matter how hard we try. The important thing about it all is whether we choose to stay down when we fall, or in faith reach for the hand of Christ, get up, and try again.

We pay, yes, for our conscious sins. Sometimes it is a case of payment deferred, but it always comes due. The medicine is administered, the spanking laid on, but even our spankings work together for good to them who love God. He is a patient, kind and just God, always ready to give us peace and a second and a twenty-second chance. Personally, I have had many spankings, and because I have, I know that God is God, and that I am His child, and that His chastisements have been administered in love.

Speaking of "child," it's time I looked after mine. Time out . . . !

17
The Bible

GOT A BIBLE in your home? Ever read it?

I'm not being facetious, ladies. I'm serious about this. I find Bibles everywhere I go, in all sorts of homes, and I like that. I read, year after year, that the Bible is still the best-seller of *all* books, and I like that. My joy is tempered a little when I hear some preacher say that this Bible is the best-sold and least-read of all books, but I'm still glad the Old Book is being distributed to such a wide audience.

What "bugs" me most is the constant evidence that our *children*, generally speaking, are not as well acquainted with the Bible as they are with Mickey Mouse and Little Red Riding Hood. That isn't their fault; it's ours. It's supposed to be funny to hear the children display their ignorance of the Book of books—like the little girl who told Art Linkletter that Alice in Wonderland was her favorite Bible story, or the boy who answered, in a quiz, the question "What are the Epistles?" by saying that the Epistles were the wives of the Apostles. It isn't funny, Magee; it's tragic.

I think it's high time we mothers really got to work on Bible reading and discussion in the home, for several reasons. One reason is that we wouldn't have the kind of homes we've got in America without the presence and influence of this Bible. From Plymouth Rock to Virginia, it was planted by our forefathers as the seed of American democracy and a new way of life on a new continent; its precepts are written into the Constitution, creeds, and customs of our land. It is good history—good *American* history. If we want our children to love and appreciate America, we had better show them early in their lives that its greatness and freedom are Bible-born.

Don't take my word for it. Listen to U. S. Grant: "The Bible is the sheet anchor of our liberties." Or to Andrew Jackson: "That Book, sir, is the rock upon which our republic rests." Patrick Henry, a rather familiar figure in the fight for American freedom, said that "The Bible is worth more than all the other books that have ever been printed." Abraham Lincoln believed it to be "the greatest gift God has ever given to men." George Washington, who knew something about government, held that it was impossible "rightly to govern the world without God and the Bible." Horace Greely thought the Bible was responsible for the rise of the common man, and the defense of his rights, in America; he said, "It is impossible to enslave mentally or socially a Bible-reading people. The principles of the Bible are the ground-work of human freedom." Need more? You'll find such tribute to the Book on the lips of any great and true American.

Yes, it's good history, and our children should know it. They will be told by some cynics, as they grow older, that there are mistakes in dates and historical events in the Bible. Of course, we can tell them that the Bible was never intended to be used as a textbook in history classrooms, but to me it seems better to tell them what Sir

Isaac Newton told us: "There are more sure marks of authenticity in the Bible than in any profane history." Yes, it's good history. It is good education in the study of man's attempt to find God, and God's attempt to reach man. Tennyson said that "Bible reading is an education in itself," and it was William Lyon Phelps who said that if he had the choice between a college student without a knowledge of the Bible, and a young man without the college education but with a good knowledge of the Bible, he would pick the latter.

It is good history, and it is good *reading*. There is no writing like it, before or since it was written. When Pearl Buck wrote her famous *Good Earth*, the finest compliment that was paid to her beautiful writing came from a hard-boiled critic who said, "It reads like the Book of Ruth!" How many of our great books have borrowed plots, titles, and characters from the Bible? The greatest of our artists and writers have read the Book for inspiration; take the influence of this Book out of literature and art, and you rob art and literature of its greatest works and its noblest expressions, of the sound of music that began with the singing of David's Psalms by lonely shepherds on the Galilean hills.

It's good reading, yes, as well as good history—and yet, if this were *all* it is, it wouldn't mean too much to me. It wasn't written to be read as "good literature"; it was written to guide men to God, to lift them from sin and ugly living into abundant life built on the model of the Master. I read in a magazine the other day these arresting words by an unknown author: "The Bible, God's Holy Word, is not to be read like any other book, or like a newspaper, or a magazine; too many blessings are lost unless it is read as a personal message from God

Himself." That's it! *That is why we should read it.* You wouldn't refuse to read a letter from your best friend, would you? And if God be your Best Friend, and has something to say to you—?

The Bible is a text on good and godly living. It is "The Book of Life," an account of the noblest Life ever lived upon this earth. It is a continued story of the lifting up of man from the days when brother could kill brother in cold blood and feel no pangs of conscience to the day when Jesus said, "Love your enemies, bless them that curse you, do good to them that hate you, and pray for them which despitefully use you, and persecute you" (MATTHEW 5:44), and with that day, with this Jesus, God's love began to rule the hearts of men, and His Way became the ideal way of life for all men everywhere.

I love this Book not because it is good history and good reading; I love it because I see it as God's holy broom sweeping clean the hearts of mankind. I have seen it turn liars into truth-tellers, thieves into benefactors, frustrated people into men and women seeking and following the purpose and plan of the Almighty, proud fools into humble saints. I love it because I know it to be the most powerful force in the changing and ennobling of human life that has ever existed anywhere. It has changed *me*, and that is all the evidence I need as to its power. It works.

There was a British skeptic who said once that it was impossible these days to believe in any book whose authority was "unknown." A Christian asked him if he knew the name of the compiler of the multiplication table. He said he did not. "Then, of course, you don't believe in it?" Replied the skeptic, "Of course, I believe

110

in it. It works." Said the Christian, "So does the Bible." And the skeptic said nothing.

Why do we cheat our children of a thorough knowledge of such a mighty Book? Would we refuse to give them necessary medicine, if they were sick, to make them well? Would we refuse a man dying in the desert a cup of cold water? Do you refuse your child food for his body? Of course, you don't. *But what about food for his heart, mind, and soul?*

There are things in the Bible that I do not understand, but if I waited until I understood all of it I would never get any good out of any of it. Dr. S. Parkes Cadman was asked once if he thought all of the Bible of equal value; he replied, "When you eat fish, you don't eat bones and all, do you?" Think that over, carefully. I "eat" what I can understand, and enjoy it; I leave what I cannot understand to the God who inspired the Bible. He knows, and I am content to leave it there. I agree with Mark Twain, who said once that it wasn't the parts of the Bible he couldn't understand that bothered him; it was the parts he *could* understand. And with the man who said, "Men do not reject the Bible because it contradicts *itself*, but because it contradicts *them*."

It contradicts all that is unworthy in my life; it contradicts my greed, my selfishness, my ignoble ambitions. It contradicts the worst in me and encourages the best. It makes me lift my sights to God. It makes a "new creature" of me, through its Christ. A Mohammedan trader in India asked a European friend to get him a "European" Bible. Asked why, when he could not read any European language, he replied, "When a ship brings a European trader to me who is a stranger to me and who wants to trade with me, I put the Bible in his way and watch him.

If he opens it and reads it, I know I can trust him. But if he throws it aside with a sneer or a curse, I will have nothing to do with him, because I know I cannot trust him." Exactly!

A famous translator of the classics, having translated Homer's *Odyssey* and *Iliad*, decided to write a new translation of the four Gospels. His son said, "It will be interesting to see what Father makes of the Gospels. It will be more interesting to see what the Gospels make of Father!" Wise boy! No one but God knows what the Bible can make of us—and of our children.

18
Life

TIME OUT, LADIES: let's "sum up." The last chapter of a book like this is supposed to do just that—to sort of "pull it together," to re-emphasize the central theme of what we've been writing about. That's difficult, here, for we've been talking about a lot of different things, but there may be one word that describes it all: we've been talking about *life*.

Life is pretty important: we only live once on this earth, and when that's over, it's over—so, as I've said before, we'd better make the most of it while we've got it. As the poet said, "We shall not pass this way again." It's hard, making the most of it, because most of us don't really know what life *is*. Balzac called it "the human comedy." Cynical H. L. Mencken said that the basic fact about life "is not that it is a tragedy, but that it is a bore." (Maybe for you, Mr. Mencken, but not for me!) Herman Melville was more intelligent about it when he said, "Life's a voyage that's homeward bound." That I like. Barrie said, "Life is a long lesson in humility," and I can go for that, too.

I have known the time when life was a dreary business, when it didn't make sense, when it all seemed so useless. I was a sad case, and making a mess of life. I was insecure, vain, self-centered, constantly looking for peace in my soul, and there was no peace. Then one morning I knelt in the prayer-room of a church, and life came to me: *Jesus Christ came to me*, and I gave myself to Him, and in that instant life was no longer dreary, but wonderful, and it has been, ever since.

For, you see, Christ *is* life. He said so Himself: "I am the way, the truth, *and the life* . . ." (JOHN 14:6). Life came to me, as I had never known it before; the Holy Spirit came into my heart and illuminated and glorified everything. I was made clean and filled with a new Spirit, and given purpose and direction in my life—and a peace that passes all understanding. If that's what you're looking for, look to Jesus Christ, and find it!

I call Him wonderful, just as the Prophet Isaiah called Him: ". . . and his name shall be called Wonderful . . ." (ISAIAH 9:6). Out here in Hollywood, we go for big words in ballyhooing our product—words like "gigantic," "colossal," "stupendous," "horrendous," "electrifying," "marvelous," "fabulous," "fantastic." But never in human history has anyone been so beautifully and perfectly described as our Lord Jesus Christ, and by this one word: "wonderful"! He is wonderful to the point of miracle. My dictionary defines miracle as "A person, thing, or event that causes astonishment and admiration and awe, aroused by something strange, unexpected, incredible. . . . A wondrous happening that is contrary to or independent of the known laws of nature. . . ."

He is wonderful to me. He is my whole life, my prime reason for living, for keeping on even when everything seems to be going against me. He is wonderful to me because He is the fleshly manifestation of the fullness of the glory of God *reborn within me*. He has touched my life with His glory; I need no further "evidence" of His

114

deity and power. I know, because I have experienced it.

Consider the wonders of Jesus Christ.

There is the wonder of His birth. He was born not in the palace of a king, but in the stable of an inn, in a manger surrounded by lowly animals and startled humans. He through whom they were created came, a smaller creature than they! No other birthplace in our world is so filled with meaning and awe.

There is the wonder of the announcement of His birth —the singing of the heavenly hosts to the shepherds in the fields, the great light breaking, the star that guided the wise men, the wonder in which "they departed into their own country [by] another way" (MATTHEW 2:12). When they came to Bethlehem they walked through a world of fear and incredulity; but when they went away from the manger the road was different—everything and everyone along the way was alight with the glory and the wonder of God lying there in the manger in the form of a human child.

There is the wonder of His childhood. The Son of God was obedient to Mary and Joseph, as the Commandment demanded; He through whom they were created became a child, obedient to them. "Honor thy father and thy mother . . ."; that took on new, wonderful meaning in the Child Christ.

As a Child of twelve He astounded the scholars and the "doctors" in the temple with His understanding and wisdom and knowledge of the law. Never before had they seen or heard a Child like this! Within Him there was something they had seen in no other child; it was not human, but superhuman, supernatural, divine. He left them staring, wondering.

There is the wonder of His growth in maturity and

wisdom. He could have come into the world as a full-grown man, as a powerful king with armies of angels, and the world would have fallen on its face before Him. But no—He came to live as a Boy among other boys, that He might better understand and teach them, and help them grow in maturity and wisdom—as He has helped me.

There is the wonder of His first miracle: the turning of water into wine at the wedding feast in Cana of Galilee. I understand it was the custom in those days that the eldest son should provide the wine for such a feast, and if the eldest son could not be present or could not do it, then the next son in line should do it. Jesus' mother came to Him and said there was no wine, suggesting thereby that He should do something about it. He said, "Woman, what have I to do with thee? mine hour is not yet come" (JOHN 2:4). He meant no disrespect; actually He was showing His respect for Jewish custom in reminding His mother that it wasn't His "turn," or place, to do this. Yet He obeyed her and provided the wine. He does the same thing for us when He takes a dreary, anemic life, washes it with His blood, and makes it rich with the "wine" of the Spirit.

There is the wonder of His compassion for those who suffered from sin, guilt, sickness, and death. He healed men, women, and children of all sorts of diseases. He raised their loved ones from the dead. He calmed the storms that raged in their souls. He fed the five thousand. He showed His fishermen-disciples how to cast their nets, telling them to launch out into the deep; He has made net-casters of all who love Him, and made them launch out into the deeps of life, unafraid.

There is the wonder of His indignation at those who

denied God and persecuted His people. He drove out the money-changers from the temple; He saved the life of the poor woman taken in adultery and sent her self-appointed executioners away in shame at *their* sin. He put within all of us a divine and holy anger, not at men, but at the tendencies in men to deny God and His commandments.

There is the wonder of His silence before Pilate. He could have called down legions of angels to defend Him, but He would not. He knew what Pilate did not know: that through the cross to which Pilate sent Him, He would lift all men unto Him. He would not argue with Pilate; He was certain of what He was doing, and Pilate was only afraid. His word on the cross, "Father, forgive them; for they know not what they do" (LUKE 23:34), included Pilate.

There is the wonder of his resurrection. He had promised that He would arise from the dead, and He did. None other in history has so promised and so arisen. I cannot doubt that He arose. Too many saw Him—after Calvary and the tomb. He has arisen in *me*. I do not argue about the resurrection; I am its witness.

Last of all, but not least, the wonder of His last command: "Go ye into all the world, and preach the gospel to every creature. He that believeth and is baptized shall be saved . . ." (MARK 16:15–16). That means us. This means me, and it is why I am saying in this chapter that for me life is doing just that.

So there it is. There, I think, is the wonder, and the meaning, and the peace that so many of us seek and miss because we never quite understand that Christ is Life—the only Life worth living. I am appalled by the vast number of people who seek and never find—because they seek in the wrong direction, or give up seeking, entirely. There are millions of women living idle, fruitless, inconsequent, and bitter lives in America, hunting peace and satisfaction and purpose in charity drives and country clubs and *everywhere* but at the one source that can give them what they so desperately long for and forever miss. They will never, never "hit the top" until they live like Him and in Him, and He in them. He made you an offer, long ago: "I am come that they might have life, and that they might have it more abundantly" (JOHN 10:10). You'll never get it without Him; you will never know peace, nor fulfillment.

Two Arabs came into Cairo and got a room at a hotel. It was their first experience in such a place. They became fascinated with the faucets in their room that produced endless streams of water. When they left, they tore the two magical faucets from the wall and made off with them, thinking that the disconnected gadgets would give them water in their desert!

We know better. We are so much wiser! We understand that to obtain the blessed, nourishing, all-important "waters of life," we must be attached to the source of supply. Or *do* we know it? How many of us become attached to the source, and *stay* attached?

Time out, ladies, for Christ—all the time you have, if you would really *live*.